THE UNIVERSITY OF MICHIGAN
CENTER FOR CHINESE STUDIES

MICHIGAN MONOGRAPHS IN CHINESE STUDIES
NO. 45

CHINESE SOCIAL AND ECONOMIC HISTORY FROM THE SONG TO 1900

Report of the American Delegation
to a Sino-American Symposium,
Beijing, 26 October-1 November 1980

edited by

Albert Feuerwerker

Ann Arbor

Center for Chinese Studies
The University of Michigan

1982

Library of Congress Cataloging in Publication Data

Chinese social and economic history from the Song
to 1900.
(Michigan monographs in Chinese studies; no. 45)
1. China—History—Congresses. 2. Sino-American
Symposium on Chinese Social and Economic History from
the Song to 1900 (Peking, China: 1980).
I. Feuerwerker, Albert. II. Sino-American Symposium
on Chinese Social and Economic History from the Song to
1900 (Peking, China: 1980). III. Series.
DS702.C48   1983   951   83-1789
ISBN 0-89264-045-6

Special thanks are due the National Endowment for the Humanities, which provided the
funds to support American participation in this
binational symposium.

Printed in the United States of America

N 106

CONTENTS

PART I:
ESSAYS BY THE AMERICAN PARTICIPANTS

THE 1980 SINO-AMERICAN HISTORY SYMPOSIUM: HOW IT WAS PLANNED, ORGANIZED, AND RUN

Albert Feuerwerker

The Sino-American Symposium on Chinese Social and Economic History from the Song to 1900, which was held in Beijing from 26 October to 1 November 1980, was, I believe, the first of its kind. So far as I am aware, no such scholarly conference occurred before 1949. Given the prewar state of American studies of China's social and economic history, such an event would have been highly unlikely. It is possible that similar meetings were held by Chinese and Soviet scholars in the 1950s, but details are not readily available. Particularly in the last few years, a small number of foreign historians, including some Americans, have participated in historical meetings organized by the Chinese primarily for their own scholars.[1] The present symposium, however, was genuinely a joint undertaking by Chinese and American historians in every respect: planning, participation, organization, financing, and, above all, in the open, lively, and intensive exchange of scholarly views which characterized its sessions.

---

[1] American historians, for example, attended conferences in the People's Republic of China on the Taiping Movement, the 1911 Revolution, and Ming-Qing history among others in 1980 and 1981. (Conferences on modern economic history, Qing history, Republican China, and the 1911 Revolution with substantial American participation were also held in Taiwan from 1977 through 1981.) An international symposium on Shang civilization sponsored by the CSCPRC was held in Hawaii in September 1982.

Previous reports by delegations of historians who visited China under the auspices of the CSCPRC are: Frederic Wakeman, Jr., ed., *Ming and Qing Historical Studies in the People's Republic of China*, China Research Monograph no. 17 (Berkeley: University of California, Institute of East Asian Studies, 1980); and Ying-shih Yü, ed., *Early Chinese History in the People's Republic of China* (Seattle: University of Washington, School of International Studies, 1981). See also Anne F. Thurston and Jason H. Parker, eds., *Humanistic and Social Science Research in China: Recent History and Future Prospects* (New York: Social Science Research Council, 1980).

The symposium took place within the framework of the agreements on scholarly exchanges concluded between, on the American side, the Committee on Scholarly Communication with the People's Republic of China (of the National Academy of Sciences, Social Science Research Council, and American Council of Learned Societies) and, on the Chinese side, the Chinese Academy of Social Sciences and the Chinese Academy of Sciences. Travel costs to China for the ten American participants and the expenses of a planning meeting (as well as costs incurred by the translation of the American papers into Chinese and the duplication of the American and Chinese papers for distribution to the participants prior to the symposium) were borne by the CSCPRC. The costs of the meeting itself, all the expenses of the Chinese participants, and the expenses of the ten American participants were the responsibility of the Chinese Academy of Social Sciences. The National Endowment for the Humanities generously provided financial support to the CSCPRC for the purposes of this symposium.

In November 1979, while in China with a CSCPRC delegation to negotiate scholarly exchanges, Professor Frederic Wakeman of the University of California at Berkeley, then vice-chairman of the CSCPRC, first discussed the general topic of the symposium with representatives of the Chinese Academy of Social Sciences (CASS) and of its Institute of Historical Research (the organization primarily concerned with China's premodern history, the other two CASS history institutes being the Institute of Modern History and the Institute of World History). Early in 1980, I was asked by the CSCPRC to serve as chairman of the American delegation and to form a planning committee with Professor Wakeman and Professor Frederick Mote of Princeton University. The committee's task was to develop specific ideas for the content and organization of the symposium and to select the American participants.

By pooling our admittedly limited knowledge of contemporary Chinese scholarship and comparing that with what we knew of current American research and researchers, we drew up a list of topics that we believed might be usefully discussed by Chinese and American historians. Something of the scope of our original, more comprehensive list is reflected in the topics of the ten sessions that were actually held in Beijing (see the daily schedule of meetings, appendix B). Then came the very difficult task of selecting the American participants, who, because of financial constraints on both the Chinese and American sides, could number only nine in addition to myself. With a thousand years of Chinese history to cover and an enormous range of disciplinary competencies as well, my confidence in the high quality of the scholars who made up our delegation was amply confirmed in the course of the symposium itself. In addition to the ten "official" participants who prepared papers, four other American historians already in China conducting research with grants from the

CSCPRC attended the symposium sessions and other activities as observers and contributed importantly to the daily discussions.

On the Chinese side, we were told, a planning committee similar to our own was established. It was chaired by Professor Yan Zhongping, vice-director of the CASS Institute of Economics and a noted economic historian. Its two other members were Professor Deng Guangming, an important Song historian and at that time chairman of the history department of Beijing University, and Professor Lin Ganquan, the vice-director of the CASS Institute of Historical Research. This committee, in consultation with others, selected the twenty official Chinese participants, i.e., those who prepared papers to be discussed at the symposium. Apparently, the selection procedure involved some kind of national competition which chose the best papers from among a larger number submitted (though this procedure was closely tied to other criteria, among them geographic representation and age spread, of which more will be said below). Ten additional Chinese historians participated in the symposium as official observers, counterparts of the four American official observers. In practice, perhaps a dozen other Chinese scholars, beyond the thirty given some formal status, attended the sessions either regularly or from time to time.

We did not learn the names of the Chinese participants until late in the summer of 1980. In the meantime, it was necessary to reach agreement with the Chinese side on the precise scholarly content of the symposium and its format. Armed with our proposed list of topics, the names of the American participants, and procedural suggestions which the American planning committee had drawn up, I traveled to Beijing in May 1980 to meet with Professors Yan, Deng, and Lin and representatives of CASS. My reception was gracious and helpful, and the meeting went remarkably well.

Agreement was quickly reached on the range of topics to be discussed at the symposium. I made three other substantive suggestions to my Chinese colleagues. On these matters, too, which we considered at some length, we were able rather easily to arrive at an agreement.

My first suggestion was that the symposium papers be distributed to all the participants prior to the meeting, by no later than early September. Abstracts would be prepared and distributed as soon as possible so that each side would be informed about what the other side was doing. The papers were to be twenty to thirty pages in length, with those by the Chinese participants to be distributed only in Chinese and those by the Americans to be written in English and provided with Chinese translations. (In general, the Chinese participants knew little English—there were exceptions, of course—while all of the Americans could read Chinese reasonably well.) As the papers would all have been read prior to the symposium, at the daily sessions the authors would present only brief opening remarks. These were to be followed, as each paper was discussed in turn, by substantial critiques offered by critics designated beforehand,

Chinese for the American papers and Americans for the Chinese papers. The critics' comments would be followed by open discussion by all the formal and informal participants. In fact, these arrangements worked reasonably well, as I explain below.

Second, the Chinese side took note of our earnest hope that their delegation include scholars of all ages and a reasonable number from outside of Beijing and indicated that this was their intention. As of the time of the symposium, the ages of the twenty formal Chinese participants were as follows: 73, 70, 70, 63, 63, 59, 49, 47, 45, 43, 43, 42, 41, 41, 40, 38. The ages of the ten formal American participants, by comparison, were: 55, 52, 50, 48, 42, 42, 41, 38, 37, 37. The locations of the universities or research institutes with which the thirty Chinese scholars were affiliated were: Beijing, 18; Shanghai, 2; Xiamen, 2; Henan, 2; Guangzhou, 2; Nanjing, 1; Jilin, 1; Hebei, 1; and Sichuan, 1. (One reason, perhaps, for the preponderance of Beijing participants was the fact that the official observers, for reasons of economy, were mainly from that city.) The fourteen Americans were affiliated with institutions in the following states: California, 4; Connecticut, 2; Pennsylvania, 2; Michigan, 1; Ohio, 1; New Jersey, 1; Massachusetts, 1; Hawaii, 1; and London, England, 1 (not a state, of course!).

Third, the Chinese side, while noting the extremely difficult housing situation in Beijing (for transients as well as permanent residents), agreed to try to arrange for the American and Chinese delegations to live and eat together during the course of the symposium. I do believe that a good faith effort was made—the Chinese delegates coming from outside of Beijing were told that all of us would be lodged together—but the clout of CASS was insufficient to the task. Possibly the space that CASS had hoped to use was preempted by organizations that could claim greater priority. As it happened, the Americans were comfortably housed and fed in a former cadre hostel, the Yanshan Binguan, located in the northwest of Beijing near People's University. The Chinese delegation stayed at the Jiguan Zhaodaisuo, a hostel belonging, I believe, to the State Council and located in the center of the city. It was here, too, in very pleasant circumstances, that the daily sessions of the symposium were held. Unfortunately, commuting between hotel and meeting place by the American delegation consumed two hours daily. Though not as many as we had hoped, there were still a number of opportunities for informal meetings between members of the two delegations: before and after each session, in the thirty-minute break halfway through each session, at two banquets (one hosted by each side), at two informal lunches that we shared, during one evening of informal discussions, and at the fine "cocktail party" given by CASS at the close of the symposium.

The American delegation met in Washington at the beginning of June 1980 to hear the results of my discussions in Beijing, to work out in detail individual assignments and responsibilities, and to discuss its postsymposium itinerary in China (mainly academic meetings in cities other than Beijing, but also visits to historic sites—this was the first visit to the PRC for five of the American participants). In general, most of the abstracts and papers were in fact exchanged and distributed prior to the symposium, so that we arrived in Beijing in late October prepared to proceed in the manner outlined above. I would be remiss if I did not here mention the very able staff assistance provided by Ms. Patricia Tsuchitani of the CSCPRC. And special tribute is due Professor Robert Hartwell for suggesting how the thirty papers might be grouped for efficient discussion of related topics.

In addition to the formal opening session on 26 October—with speeches by Huan Xiang, vice-president of the Chinese Academy of Social Sciences, and myself which were widely reported in the Chinese press and on the radio, and where we were greeted also by Wang Guangmei, foreign secretary of CASS—the symposium consisted of ten three-and-one-half-hour sessions spread over six days (two days being scheduled to permit free afternoons). Most authors in fact managed to confine themselves to the ten-minute introductions they were allowed, the designated discussants or critics were well prepared, and the discussions provoked by these opening comments were extremely difficult to contain within the three-and-one-half-hour format since three papers were discussed at each session. Those who wished to speak during the discussion period wrote their names on a blackboard at the front of the room; they were then recognized in turn by the chairman of the day, who usually took some liberties in an attempt to allow comments on the same subject to follow each other consecutively. With a few exceptions, no comments or questions were raised spontaneously from the floor.

The dominant language of the discussions was Chinese, but comments were made in both Chinese and English and in each case were translated in full or in summary by one of the three official interpreters who were present at all times or by one of the bilingual members of the two delegations. Even those American participants who did not speak Chinese well understood that language to some degree. Some of the Americans prepared comments in Chinese in advance or spontaneously concocted translations of their remarks. The assistance of the Chinese-Americans among the formal and informal American participants was of critical importance in assuring that communication proceeded smoothly and accurately. Some of the other Americans spoke Chinese reasonably well; the rest of us were aware of our enormous linguistic shortcomings.

While the designated discussants of the Chinese papers were Americans, and vice versa, in the discussions themselves no such national lines were observed. Both the Chinese and American participants commented freely, and often eagerly, in support or in criticism of the interpretations or data of

Chinese and American papers and of the comments made by other participants. It is, I believe, something of an achievement that we were able to hold
the symposium in a format which omitted the practice, quite common at
Chinese academic meetings, of reading the papers in full during the plenary
sessions. Thirty working hours for thirty papers was already much too short.
Many of those who wished to comment at a particular session or to join the
discussion more than once were unable to do so. And, I note, this was not
simply because there were too many papers for the time available. More
importantly, the symposium was characterized by genuine and intense intellectual interchange which was only partly constrained by the contrast between
Chinese ideological commitment, on the one hand, and American eclecticism,
on the other.

Relatively full news reports of the symposium appeared in *Renmin ribao*
and *Guangming ribao* and in Xinhua News Agency dispatches, and an extensive
summary of the contents of the discussions was published in *Guangming ribao*
on 9 December 1980. This volume reprints the fullest Chinese report on the
symposium, which appeared originally in *Social Sciences in China*.

The brief essays by the American participants which form the first part of
this report discuss our impressions of the symposium, of the abilities and interests of our Chinese colleagues, and of the current state of Chinese studies of
China's premodern economic and social history. Professor G. William Skinner,
the vice-chairman of our delegation, graciously undertook to organize the
preparation of the abstracts of the American and Chinese papers presented at
the symposium which form the second part of this report. The appendixes
contain schedules, namelists, and brief descriptions (prepared by Professor
Jerry Dennerline) of two major libraries which, I believe, we were the first
American scholars to visit.

Our brief personal essays are not intended to be comprehensive analyses of
the Chinese historical scene, even for the brief period at the end of 1980 when
we had an opportunity to view it. And the last two years have seen a prolifera-
tion of books and articles on all aspects of China's history, including those that
were the subjects of our symposium. The main outlines of this work can be
followed, for example, in *Zhongguo lishixue nianjian 1979* [Yearbook of Chinese
history] (Beijing, 1980) and *Zhongguo lishixue nianjian 1980* (Beijing, 1982). Our
tentative "cross section" will therefore in some respects be quickly out of
date. But we hope, nevertheless, that we have been able to record accurately
the positive but not uncritical response to our Chinese colleagues and their
work that will be the basis for fruitful and enhanced scholarly cooperation in
the future.

I shall close with a personal view of what I see as the most important
intellectual difference between Chinese and American scholarship in the area
of social and economic history, a difference that was underscored but, of

course, not revealed for the first time by the symposium. This is the predisposition of Chinese historians to concentrate their attention almost exclusively on the question of why China's "feudal" society and economy did not develop, as the normative Marxist paradigm would have it, into industrial capitalism; why it remained stagnant at, at best, a "semifeudal, semicolonial" stage wherein promising "sprouts of capitalism" foundered. The problem of nondevelopment or underdevelopment is not a trivial one. On the other hand, it was the common condition of most of humankind until the very recent past, and the failure to achieve industrial modernity—far from being a major intellectual puzzle—is overdetermined by the variety of cultural, political, economic, and social analyses that have been elaborated by scholarship in many countries in recent decades. It is much more difficult to state precisely why and how the first generation of industrial nations (beginning with England and then spreading to parts of Western Europe, North America, and Japan) achieved their development than it is to understand why the others did not. (Not to be facetious, this historical problem parallels the contemporary practical difficulties faced by China and other nations which are striving to bring about modern economic growth.)

Prior to the Industrial Revolution, China's premodern economic growth, and the remarkable cultural achievements of Chinese civilization, were anything but "underdeveloped." If we use that term at all, it has more meaning when applied to Europe before, say, 1700 than it does to Song, Ming, and early Qing China. The emphasis of American scholarship on premodern China, in contrast to the Chinese orientation, has been one of attempting to understand how that society and economy was organized and how it functioned, what was the structure and pattern of premodern growth. While we have undoubtedly benefited from our increasing ability to utilize the conceptual and methodological tools of the social sciences, American historians have been constrained by their linguistic shortcomings and by limited access to primary source materials which are available only in China. And they have not always been helped by the quite different approaches taken in the work of their Chinese counterparts, whom one would reasonably expect to make the major contributions to the understanding of their own past.

If Chinese historians, for example, do not proceed beyond responding ambiguously to the development of trade and commerce—on the one hand, there is an eager search for early manifestations of "capitalism," but at the same time commerce is described as exploiting the peasantry and is feared because it might lead to capitalism—they are in fact failing to probe very deeply into the structure and functioning of China's premodern economy and society. Evaluations of the past properly come later, and it is indeed only the Chinese, who, in the last analysis, can pass judgment on their own history, but first it is necessary to comprehend in empirical and analytical terms precisely how the complex marketing institutions which articulated China's remarkable millenium of premodern economic growth actually operated.

Explicit or not, there is, of course, a hidden agenda to all of the writing of history that we undertake, Chinese and Americans included. This was apparent at the symposium to those who had followed the development of the relationship between Chinese historiography and Chinese politics during the past thirty years. And contemporary commentary is in no way a dishonorable part of the historian's profession—from Sima Qian and Thucydides to the Cliometricians and the *Annales* school—but it is only a part, however much to be honored. There is a different kind of relevance, though I believe strongly that it is still of the utmost contemporaneity, in the attempt to understand the human past in all of its remarkable manifestations. Perhaps it is only a wish, but I do conclude that the present symposium brought us not a few important steps further along the road of Chinese and American cooperation in this endeavor.

CHINESE HISTORY AND THE SOCIAL SCIENCES

G. William Skinner

Perhaps the most striking contrast between Chinese and American historical scholarship as evidenced at the Beijing symposium concerns their intellectual stance toward the social sciences. Most of the American papers were to some degree informed by social science. They contained references to the works of sociologists, social anthropologists, economists, political scientists, demographers, or human geographers. They used models and concepts drawn from these disciplines and to some extent adopted the problem-oriented stance characteristic of social science research. The Chinese papers, by contrast, drew little inspiration from these other disciplinary traditions. Their references to secondary literature were almost exclusively to the work of other historians, and their intellectual orientation was quite strictly historiographic if not historicist.

This particular contrast would not have been drawn thirty years ago. At that time, history was innocent of social science in the West no less than in China. The gap between the two national groups of historians that has developed during the past thirty years should not be chalked up to the socialist reorientation of history in China: it was, rather, a consequence of transformations within Western academia. During recent decades, Western historians have gained an appreciation of what social science has to offer, and equally important, history has been brought into the social sciences. Whole new fields have developed at the interface—historical sociology and historical demography are notable examples—and they are manned, at least in part, by scholars who are at once historians and social scientists. In a word, scholarly discourse has managed to cross disciplinary boundaries despite the professional structures that serve to strengthen them. It is not for nothing that social science history in the West is also known as multidisciplinary history.

We might well ask why no comparable development has taken place within China's history profession. Let me point to three of the more immediate "causes."

First, during most of the thirty years in question, the various social sciences in China were either repressed or neglected. Their legitimacy was called into question as early as 1952. Sociology and political science were officially expunged from universities and institutes by the mid-1950s. At the same time, the scope of social anthropology was restricted to the 6 percent of the population that was not Han Chinese. Demography, too, was ideologically suspect and lost its institutional base. In all of these fields, few if any professionals were trained from the mid-1950s to the late 1970s. While the academic standing of economics and geography was never directly compromised, both disciplines were pushed in the direction of applied, policy-oriented concerns of the present. It goes without saying that fields whose disciplinary integrity is in jeopardy are unlikely to display the intellectual vigor that might influence developments within a sister discipline.

A second factor relates to the fact that Chinese history, inevitably central to the profession in China, is only peripheral in the United States. In a sense, then, historians of China within Chinese academia had no need for extradisciplinary allies, nor was there any programmatic need for special developmental attention. The situation was quite the reverse in the United States. When in the postwar era the American establishment determined to develop academic expertise in the so-called "exotic" areas of the globe, Chinese studies—the interdisciplinary study of China—embarked on a period of vigorous growth. The institutional framework adopted was particularly felicitous. Area-studies centers in the major universities brought together area specialists from different fields and fostered an interdisciplinary approach to research. Most historians of China in the United States today were trained in such centers, where they worked as a matter of course with a variety of social scientists. Because of its favorable effect on the quality of research, the area-studies formula was eventually extended to the study of Western Europe and even the United States. Today the field of American studies flourishes, and research on the American past is fast becoming a genuinely multidisciplinary endeavor. In this sense, of course, there is no Chinese studies in China. Indeed, a comparable development would be surprising. The contrast nonetheless goes far in explaining why Chinese history in China appears parochial by contrast with the United States, where it assumes a more comparative, eclectic, and multidisciplinary guise.

The third factor I would stress in this context is communications. Scholarly discourse presumes fora and media, and in China institutional arrangements have provided few that are suitable for cross-disciplinary exchange. Prior to 1977, institutes and universities were relatively isolated from one another, both geographically and structurally. Ensconced in their Institute of Nationality Studies, anthropologists inevitably had little contact with social and economic historians. Research conferences, infrequent in any case, were almost invariably discipline-specific. By contrast, in the United States, intellectual interchange among all academic institutions is continual and widespread.

Professional societies such as the Social Science History Association and the Association for Asian Studies are in large part dedicated to the marriage of history with the social sciences. National institutes such as the Center for Advanced Study at Stanford, the Institute for Advanced Study in the Behavioral Sciences at Princeton, and the East-West Center in Honolulu are multidisciplinary in conception and operation. It is true that both China and the United States must contend with the intellectually divisive structure of departments and schools, but Chinese universities can boast few mechanisms for getting around it. For instance, the interdepartmental centers and institutes that have become a regular feature of American academia are rare in China. Above all, one must stress the importance of multidisciplinary journals. To be sure, university journals in China occasionally bring articles by historians and social scientists between the covers of the same issues, though this, one suspects, occurs less by design than by necessity. In any case, at the national level one may look in vain for counterparts of the *Journal of Interdisciplinary History*, the *Journal of Asian Studies*, or *Comparative Studies in Society and History*.

It should be clear by now that I write as an advocate of history as a social science. In the present context, then, I am suggesting that the isolation of history from the social sciences in China has had certain deleterious effects. I will make reference in very general terms to the papers prepared for the Beijing symposium by our Chinese colleagues, and to make my point I must unfairly dwell on shortcomings rather than on their considerable strengths.

Let me begin with a very specific anthropological case in point. The Chinese lineage has been the subject of much concern among anthropologists. The major analytical breakthrough was made by Maurice Freedman in 1958, and within a decade he and his intellectual successors put together a brilliant analysis of considerable theoretical significance. The value of this analysis for local historians of China was quickly perceived in the West, and the first of the major historical monographs to be informed by it appeared as early as 1966. Chinese anthropologists were no doubt capable of constructing a similar analysis, but they were prevented from doing so by the decision that put Chinese society outside the bounds of this sort of academic investigation. Thus, historians in China have no comparable analysis to draw on. With no understanding of the processes of lineage formation and segmentation or of the structural differences between localized lineages, higher-order lineages, and clans, Chinese local historians have been unable to sort out their data in any meaningful fashion. Freedman's analysis of the dialectical interaction between the lineage and the Chinese state was badly needed at the conference. Most references to lineages emphasized the interests lineage leaders shared with the state apparatus; there was too little appreciation of the ways in which the interests of lineage and state were opposed.

More fundamentally, historians in the West have, through extended contact with anthropological colleagues, incorporated in their conceptual baggage the notion of cultural relativity and a holistic perspective on human society. These were largely lacking among our Chinese colleagues. The Chinese family system was taken for granted as an existential fact, wholly unproblematic. No connection was perceived between the joint family system or partible inheritance and demographics in China. Why or how these features of Chinese society arose and the role of the state in supporting them were not perceived as problematic by Chinese social historians. At the risk of oversimplification, our Chinese colleagues lacked a comparative perspective on their own social institutions.

I detected, moreover, a conviction that ethnography was simply irrelevant to history. In my own conference paper I drew on ethnographic findings from the 1930s and 1940s to help me infer what marketing arrangements may have been in the same localities during the late nineteenth century. This procedure was denounced as anachronistic. Such methodological purity, however, flies in the face of a strategy that has generally proved rewarding in reconstructing the past: namely, to begin with a full-scale institutional analysis during a recent period for which the data base is strong and then to work back in time, on the basis of sparser data, attending always to what is known about the principles of institutional change. Ye Xian'en came close to pursuing such a strategy in his study of servile tenants in Huizhou, but his recourse to field work and ingenious use of ethnographic data, while pleasing the American participants, drew criticism from several of his Chinese colleagues. I suspect that resistance to this strategy stems in part from the sharp specialization of Chinese historians by temporal period and in part from the fact that the few empirically oriented social scientists in China have been too busy with the present to develop or pursue any interest in the past.

In the wake of this resistance to even the most timid extrapolation across historical periods, I was surprised to hear an extended ethnographic description of conditions among the Chiang (a non-Han people in northwestern Sichuan) invoked in support of a reconstruction of customs among the Han Chinese in Song times. Of course, there may have been historical interaction whereby cultural elements were borrowed both ways, but the context of these remarks at the symposium had to do with stages of development, the upshot being that the Chiang must be at the same stage in the twentieth century as Han peasants were in the Song. This kind of thinking would not pass muster with historians who had been exposed to modern anthropology.

These examples of naiveté on the side of anthropology could be matched with respect to the other social sciences, but it would be presumptuous of me to pursue the matter.

What about the prospects for a more social science-oriented history in China? Here, it seems to me, we may assume a much more upbeat stance. In some ways, China's intellectual tradition is better suited to the development of multidisciplinary history than was the West's. Classical training in China was never narrowly humanistic. The subject matter of the social sciences was always fully covered in the histories, and it was given remarkably analytical treatment. The social science journals of the 1930s and 1940s included many articles analyzing the past. Moreover, Chinese social scientists harbor no systematic bias against history, at least nothing comparable to the ideologically grounded ahistoricity of certain structural-functionalist schools in the West only a decade or so ago. Nor do Chinese historians have any particular prejudice against figures and statistics, nothing, at any rate, to match the vehemence of the American historian who as recently as 1963 warned his colleagues never to "worship at the shrine of that Bitch-goddess, QUANTIFI-CATION." In many respects, then, there are fewer hurdles to overcome than there were in the West only a scant generation ago.

For now, all depends on the fate of the social sciences in China. Only if they develop renewed vigor will their interaction with history become intellectually meaningful. And it seems to me unlikely that China's historians can get the needed exposure to social science second-hand via the works of Western historians. Policy changes since 1976 have, of course, been in the right direction. The painful process of reviving sociology and demography is now under way. Social science research has been resumed, and social scientists have reestablished ties with their colleagues abroad. History has been linked with the social sciences at the national level through the organization of the Chinese Academy of Social Sciences. In this rehabilitation effort we wish the Chinese well—for the sake of history as well as the social sciences.

SOCIAL SCIENCE HISTORY IN CHINA

Robert M. Hartwell

During the past thirty years, an increasing number of American and European scholars have adopted new approaches and techniques in their study of the past. This trend has been significant enough to lead these researchers to claim a fundamental difference between their work and a so-called "traditional" historiography. The chief distinguishing feature of the "new" social, political, and economic history has been the explicit and extensive use of the theories and methods (particularly quantitative) of the social sciences. "Social science history" has gained acceptance as the name for this new area of scholarship, particularly since 1976, when the Social Science History Association was established. The Chinese scholarly community has been largely cut off from these developments in the West. What is the present environment in China for the adoption of these approaches, and what potentialities exist for their use in the future?

Present Situation

In the West, social science history has developed on three foundations: (1) the concommitant trends whereby certain social scientists have turned their attention to historical issues and certain historians have sought training in the social science disciplines; (2) the emulation of pioneer researchers; and (3) the growing popularity of quantification (partly stimulated by the technological revolution in machine data processing), fed by an increase in the number of younger historians who receive training in statistics and quantitative analysis.

The incorporation of social science theories and methods into historical research depends on the state of these social sciences and the training of the historian. In both respects, the situation in China at the present time does not appear encouraging. Only three of the twenty formal Chinese participants in the symposium on Chinese social and economic history from the Song to 1900 had professional social science affiliations (all economics), and there was little evidence of significant social science training in the papers and discussion of the other seventeen. Three of the ten Americans, on the other hand, were professional social scientists—in the fields of law, anthropology, and sociology—and most of the others had substantial training in such disciplines as law and economics. Moreover, social science meant something different to the two groups. Previous delegations have cited the primitive state of the social sciences in China, and there is no need for me to belabor the point. I merely note that Chinese sophistication in Marxist analysis is not great, and, though better than an atheoretical Confucianism, it is still an inadequate base for the development of sophisticated social science history.

We were met with essentially the same situation at each of the various institutions we visited after the symposium. (The chief exception was in the area of historical geography, which seems to be a developing field at Fudan and Hangzhou universities—something of a surprise to us since geography departments have been on the wane in recent years in the United States.) An equally serious problem for the Chinese is the organization of their history curriculum at both the undergraduate and graduate levels. In no instance, either among the universities represented at the symposium or at any of those visited later, were programs of study in history flexible enough to allow for significant training in a social science or in statistics and quantitative analysis.

An inability to incorporate the theories and methods of the social sciences into historical research was reflected in some of the conference papers. For example, Chinese discussions of the history of economic development lacked the sophistication in economic theory that has come to be the norm in the "new" economic history in the West. The chief result was that papers on the economic issues focused on specific, highly visible phenomena without analyzing the different variables that produced such phenomena at one place at a particular time. In some papers, cities were characterized in terms of such formal criteria as size and morphology, which were seen as indicators of specific stages of development. But the authors of these pieces paid little attention to transport costs, productivity of hinterlands, urban functions, and marketing systems. Rents, wages, prices, taxes, landlord-tenant contractual arrangements, etc., were all treated as "absolutes" without any analysis that would lead someone familiar with basic economic theory to demonstrate how the "relative" significance of each variable was the result of choices between alternative possibilities. One example of this approach will suffice. It was argued that an increase in the rent for draft animals (expressed as a proportion of the animal's price) indicated an increased burden on the peasantry, but this judgment was rendered with no critical concern for the cost of feed, the price of close substitutes (e.g., the cost of human labor), alternative uses of the animals, or changes in agricultural technology.

An important stimulus to the development of social science history in the West—particularly historical studies based on prosopography or collective biography, family and demographic history, quantitative political history (electoral and legislative behavior), cliometrics, and ethnohistory—has been the emulation of the approaches and methods used in a series of pioneer studies.[1] It should be emphasized that at the beginning of the People's Republic of China in 1949, Chinese scholars were by no means completely blind to the possibilities of social science history, and the work of Fei Xiaotong, Zhang Zhongli, Wang Yuquan, and Qu Tongzu might very well be included among the pioneering studies offered as examples. But the ensuing decades in China were filled with difficulties that obstructed the development of any kind of scholarship, and the beginnings of social science history in China remained just that. Judging from conversations at the Beijing symposium, Chinese scholars have had no access to the Western studies mentioned here.

Many of the Chinese conference papers involved an analysis of quantitative data, and although their manipulation of this material was statistically crude, there was considerable reason to believe that these scholars were receptive to a more extensive use of quantification. This is not surprising—traditional Chinese historiography was far more quantitatively oriented than was true of other cultures. Moreover, it is probable that, at least at the secondary level, training in statistics and mathematics is fairly sound. The chief obstacle to the accelerated development of this aspect of social science history is access to computers and computer training. We were categorically informed that there has been absolutely no discussion among Chinese historians of putting data in machine-readable form.

Future Prospects

The chief obstacles to the progress of social science history in China are not ideological but institutional and financial. By the end of the symposium, it was clear that terms like "feudalism," "sprouts of capitalism," "landlord economy," etc., were used by many of the Chinese participants as conventional characterizations of empirical phenomena that could readily be discussed in ideologically neutral terms. But the adoption of social science methods and

---

[1] For example, Lawrence Stone, *The Crisis of the Aristocracy, 1558-1641* (Oxford, 1965); E. Le Roy Ladurie, *Les Paysans du Languedoc* (Paris, 1969); Robert W. Fogel, *Railroads and American Economic Growth* (Baltimore, 1964); Peter Temin, *Iron and Steel in Nineteenth-Century America* (Cambridge, Mass., 1964); T. K. Rabb, *Enterprise and Empire: Merchant and Gentry Investment in the Expansion of England, 1575-1730* (Cambridge, Mass., 1967); Charles Tilly, *The Vendee* (Cambridge, Mass., 1964); and the studies of Peter Laslett, W. O. Aydelotte, Lee Benson, Allan Bogue, and Jan Vansina.

theories, the emulation of and improvement upon pioneer approaches used in Western scholarship, and the development of quantitative historical analysis all face serious institutional and financial problems.

One important stimulus to the development of social science history in China is increased contact with Western historians and better access to the results of their research, not only on China but also on their own and other societies. The symposium represents a very significant beginning in this regard. It should be followed by joint workshops, conferences, symposia, and seminars in the United States, Europe, and China on specific topics in Chinese social and economic history, on comparisons between the history of China and that of other societies, and also on topics limited to European and American history. There should be a conscious effort on both sides to include the *most appropriate* PRC and Western scholars in such activities. But the availability of funds for such purposes in both China and the West has drastically limited the volume and pace of this effort. "Most appropriate" precludes the casual invitation of those Westerners who "happen" to be in China or those Chinese who "happen" to be in the United States, as well as those Chinese and Western scholars who are fortunate enough to be bilingual. Under these circumstances, the costs of transportation and translation are formidable obstacles. Finally, there is at least some reason to suspect that institutional arrangements in the People's Republic might at times make it difficult to apply "most appropriate" as the chief criterion for the selection of Chinese participants in such meetings.

Faculty and student exchanges might also prove to be a positive means for facilitating the growth in China of the "new" social, political, and economic history, but the extent of such programs is limited by the same factors that inhibit joint conferences. The most practicable first step is to ensure that the Chinese have access to the best social science history literature both as an end in itself and as a means of demonstrating the desirability of greater investment in other methods of accelerating contact with Western scholarship on social science history.

There is little possibility for well-rounded training of historians in the social sciences in the People's Republic of China until there are significant improvements in the quality of Chinese social science training and research and until Chinese historians (and social scientists) are convinced that such training is of sufficient value to justify changes in the established departmental boundaries and curriculum structures. There is little reason to be optimistic about this happening in the near future. On the other hand, the use of computers in sophisticated quantitative analysis of historical data is not likely to face formidable institutional opposition—once the potentialities become clear to the Chinese—but, in the absence of international cooperation, this innovation will be delayed until the computer becomes an integral part of university campuses the extent that relatively low priority areas such as historical research can obtain access to the equipment on a regular basis.

The chief obstacles to the development of social science history in China, then, are: (1) the present weak state of the social sciences; (2) institutional arrangements that obstruct interdisciplinary study and research in the colleges and universities; (3) the primitive state of mechanisms that might facilitate communication between historians and social scientists in China and their Western counterparts; and (4) the wherewithal that would finance the programs needed to remove these barriers. Fortunately, intellectual roadblocks to the emergence of a Chinese social science history are few, and we may hope that as economic development proceeds, investment in the social sciences and social science history will be increased to levels that may ensure steady development.

LOCAL HISTORY IN CHINA

Jerry Dennerline

It has been characteristic of Chinese social history to describe social structure in a given period without much reference to local situations. This trend has developed along with the academic institutions that support social historians. Universities and research institutes are located in major cities. Faculties and researchers are recruited from the pool of university-educated historians. It is not surprising, therefore, that academic institutions tend to sponsor research on questions of national concern and that these questions involve the origins of social institutions that have some relevance to national character or national development. The sort of history that deals with local communities and the effects of political, economic, ecological, and demographic developments on them is rarely seen. Since it is precisely this latter sort of history that is producing the most important scholarly results in the United States and Europe just now, it seems appropriate to report on the relevance of local history to Chinese scholarship as we observed it on this trip.

I will begin with a brief analysis of the importance of local situations in the issues raised by the Chinese papers at the symposium, followed by a description of the sources and methods employed by those Chinese historians whose topics were most localized. I will then examine briefly the sources for local history and their accessibility at the various archives, libraries, museums, and university centers we visited, including my assessment of the interest in local history among nonacademic people—curators, historical society members, and so on—in specific localities. Finally, I will note some of the recent studies, reprints, and published collections of documents that we were given, told about, or discovered during our travels.

No fewer than ten of the papers presented by Chinese historians at the symposium and six of the papers by members of the American delegation focused primarily on issues of social organization and social conflict. Some dealt specifically with local context as an important component of the analysis. Li Xun discussed the unusual strength of collective interests in the lower Yangzi region in the sixteenth and seventeenth centuries. Yang Guozhen's documents on land sales were all from northern Fujian and dated from the sixteenth to the nineteenth centuries. Ye Xian'en studied class relations in two villages in Huizhou prefecture, Anhui. Cheng Yingliu dealt with specific cities in the Song period. Chen Zhen focused on the city of Kaifeng during the Song. Wang Yuquan raised the issue of empirical investigation of class relations. Qi Xia discussed the development of rental contracts in the Song. Lin Renchuan focused on the issue of the southeastern coastal regional economy and class relations within it. Hong Huanchun's study dealt with labor relations in the Yangzi delta only, and Cong Hanxiang described the development of cotton growing and the spinning and weaving industries county by county in the northeast during the Ming period. Among the American delegates, Skinner, Hartwell, Rozman, and Rawski all dealt with fundamental issues of social organization, and Chen and Dennerline described sources and methods for local history.

Of the ten Chinese papers dealing with social organization and social conflict, only five stressed the local situation in their methodology. Li Xun isolated the lower Yangzi region in his analysis as a special case worth examining for its advanced level of development but did not focus on critical social developments in any particular community. Chen Zhen's paper described basic social issues in Kaifeng during the Song but introduced no new sources, methods, or interpretations. Yang Guozhen used a large number of land sale documents and limited his analysis to the region from which they came. Ye Xian'en deliberately chose to concentrate on local situations, and his analysis was based on field work in the two villages studied. Hong Huanchun's paper was based on a collection of inscriptions gathered in Suzhou by a research group working under his direction at Nanjing University. The papers by Yang, Ye, and Hong represent the segment of academic scholarship most closely related to the sort of local historical research that currently occupies most social historians in the United States and Europe.

It is perhaps significant that the papers by Yang and Ye were more concerned with description and less with analysis than were some of the papers that treated broader topics. The amount of social detail in them, on the other hand, is much more than in these more general analytical papers. Hong's paper mixed analysis with description quite freely but did not marshal evidence for the argument so much as provide description for it. If the symposium is at all representative of scholarly trends in China, these observations may be significant. First of all, Hong Huanchun was one of the more senior scholars in attendance and represented the dynamic and ambitious history faculty of Nanjing University. The project he described in his paper is representative of the trend toward publication of new documentary evidence for research. Hong's interpretation is not new, but the localized focus of the research is. It is also significant that the Nanjing history department is training its students to do field research in the lower Yangzi region, and we should expect to see increasingly interesting results of this effort as those students mature. Yang and Ye, on the other hand, were among the youngest members of the Chinese delegation. Their work is just beginning to appear in print. If they are representative, then we should expect more and more thorough descriptions based on new evidence from documents and field work, with at best a cautious approach to interpretation. Ye is a lecturer in history at Zhongshan University and thus quite far removed from the place in which he did his field work; Yang is a lecturer at Xiamen University, a student of Fu Yiling's and, like Lin Renchuan, part of what seems to be developing into one of the most important regional history projects.

Another point worth noting about these three papers in particular is that each involved the collection of data not already part of the academic or archival store. In Ye Xian'en's case, it involved independent field research using oral history; the project was begun before the Cultural Revolution but was only recently completed. In the cases of the Nanjing and Xiamen history projects, data assembly involved copying inscriptions and collecting land sale contracts within the regions in which the universities are located. Similar work is going on in Sichuan—Ran Guangrong of Sichuan University described at the symposium a recent interdisciplinary team trip to aboriginal areas—and apparently at Wuhan, although the latter university was not represented at our meetings. It might be anticipated, therefore, that more sophisticated local historical studies with some regional accent will appear as part of the academic competition between the provincial universities and the centers of scholarship in Beijing.

During the three weeks following the symposium we visited a number of institutions and met a number of people who have some interest in local historical research. I believe it is important to note that universities, research institutes, and archives do not have a monopoly on historical research. A comparison of the academic and nonacademic interests in history that we observed as we went along is therefore worthwhile. Some of the institutions we visited have been described in earlier reports. I will discuss only the problems of sources and access as they are related to the study of local history.

The Number One Archive in Beijing (Diyi, or Ming-Qing Dang'an) is becoming more accessible to Chinese scholars. It is, of course, a collection of imperial administrative documents only, but one point is worth mentioning in relation to local history. The *neiwufu* (imperial household) collection includes *huangce* (yellow registers) and *yulintuce* (fish-scale registers) for banner estates (*zhuangdou*)--documents that may be useful for localized demographic studies. Problems of access continue to make use of the rest of the collection difficult for the local historian, since no catalogue by date and no place or date index is available. The Qingshi Yanjiusuo (Qing History Research Center) of Renmin University has produced some material and organized it by date, place, and topic (see the list of publications below), and it is that institution to which we should look for increasingly sophisticated publications in this direction.

The Beijing Lishi Bowuguan (Beijing Historical Museum), which is neither an archive nor a library, holds from three to four thousand documents relevant for the study of land rights and fiscal administration. Between one and two thousand of these may date from the Ming period. Are they useful for local historians? Most, including *huangce*, *yulintuce*, lists of *jia* heads, etc., come from Huizhou prefecture (Pingyao county, Shanxi) and around Beijing. They are not yet available for researchers, though we did see some examples. Here, as elsewhere, we saw *yulintuce* from Huizhou prefecture and learned that the source for all of these was the antique market in Hangzhou. There are a good number of these records now scattered about China in university and municipal libraries, but using them for strictly local studies would be difficult since there is no catalogue and since the location of the plots described in each book is not known. There are a number of small groups *(xiaozu)* doing research at the museum; only two of these work on social-economic history, one studying land problems, the other handicraft industries.

The Number Two Archive at Nanjing includes central government documents only from 1911 to 1949. Its usefulness for local historians seems as limited as the Number One Archive, for essentially the same reasons.

Nanjing University has a *yanjiushi* (research section) for the economy of Jiangnan during the Ming and Qing dynasties. The history department library is already well known and has been used by American scholars. Copies of the Suzhou inscriptions are here, and the document collection is catalogued and open. Lü Zuoxie, a lecturer in the history department, is a living source of historical information about the city of Nanjing in the Ming period. We did not see documents or discuss sources at the Nanjing Bowuguan beyond what was exhibited there. The collection has been described in the Ming-Qing delegation's report.

The Shanghai Municipal Library has a large collection of local histories that is well known. We learned nothing new there, but we were shown some items from the collection. We did not learn of any locally significant collections elsewhere, although we visited the Hangzhou Library, the Tianyige Library in Ningbo, and the Lu Xun Museum in Shaoxing. We were unable to visit the Lu Xun Memorial Library in Shaoxing despite our requests to do so. Most startling for its lack of interest in local history was Hangzhou University, where no specialist in the history of that famous place was in evidence.

Much more interesting to the student of local history are the nonacademic institutions. Most impressive among them is the Shanghai Municipal Museum. The museum's collection of town gazetteers has also been described in the Ming-Qing report. A number of them from Shanghai municipality, most notably from the towns of Jiading county, were printed between 1961 and 1963. I was able to examine several for towns with which I am familiar. I noted that some of the social description in the gazetteer for Waigang compiled in 1631 and follow-up descriptions for the same town in a Qianlong edition, for example, is of a sort I have not seen in other sources. I imagine that these untapped sources are among the best available for local studies. Mr. Wu Guifang is in charge of the collection, and Mr. Yang Jiayu, who showed me the gazetteers, is extremely knowledgeable about their contents and local history in general. Wu's recent book on the history of Shanghai is a model of local historical description (see below).

In Jiading we visited what is claimed to be the best example of a Confucian temple, or county school, extant outside of Qufu. The building and grounds have survived and been restored to reflect the Song originals. Restoration work on the public garden outside the *pailou* (honorific arch) at the main entrance was completed just two years ago. School children visit the exhibition of Ming and Qing artifacts, which includes examples of calligraphy and painting by such local notables of the Ming and Qing periods as Li Liufang, Lou Jian, Huang Qunyue, Hou Tongzeng, Wang Jingming, Cheng Jiasui, and Qian Daxin, as well as local archaeological finds and local handicrafts. Passersby read the inscription in honor of the Ming loyalist martyrs who defended the city against the Qing invaders in 1645, and a veritable forest of stone inscriptions stands in the temple's grounds. The curator, Ms. Liu Chuyong, was trained at the Shanghai Museum and is quite knowledgeable about the county's history. She has a small staff—two or three persons working on local projects—and historical preservation seems to be the primary goal. The staff is not university-trained. Ms. Liu also told us that the museum has had some help from local members of the older generation and that some cautious attempts at assembling an oral history are under way. She has no great expectations concerning caches of family documents or the like, but the museum is known to be open to donations of any sort of material.

In Suzhou we were escorted by the curator of the local museum, Mr. Zhang Yinglin, on tours of the city and the suburbs. Mr. Zhang is very knowledgeable about Suzhou's history and was able to provide information about the history of a suburban factory as readily as he could provide information about the gardens, the location of Tang Yin's grave, and so on. Again, historical preservation is the primary interest of the museum, but Mr. Zhang told us that a detailed history of the streets of Suzhou is also being prepared.

In Shaoxing, the Lu Xun Museum preserves something of the neighborhood that Lu Xun grew up in. Unfortunately, we could not visit the library. We met three representatives of the Committee for the Preservation of Cultural Artifacts in Shaoxing County (Shaoxing Xian Wenwu Baoguan Weiyuanhui), two of whom were high-school teachers. They had no local historical projects to report. In Ningbo, on the other hand, we met several representatives of the Ningbo Historical Society (Ningbo Shi Lishi Xuehui), including teachers from the teachers' college, a high-school principal of forty years, and a former curator of the Tianyige Library. We were told that the society has fifty-four members, that it is autonomous but loosely affiliated with the Zhejiang Provincial Institute of Social Science (Zhejiang Sheng Shehui Kexue Yanjiusuo), an organization we judged to be vying for the status of "branch" of the National Academy of Social Science. Another organization, the Ningbo Region Historical Society (Ningbo Diqu Lishi Xuehui), is just getting started. It is not yet clear what these societies will do. Discussions of sources, documents, oral history, and the like did not turn up any current projects.

It is perhaps worth mentioning that the Tiantongsi, the famous Chan temple outside Ningbo that was the origin of Dogen's Soto sect, is thriving and selling highly priced copies of its own history to Japanese pilgrims. The Tianyige Library is rebuilding its collection, including gazetteers from the area, but it did not have any startling local holdings, and Mr. Qiu Sibin, the responsible person, knew of no unpublished manuscripts of town gazetteers like those at the Shanghai Museum and the Shanghai Municipal Library. The collection of genealogies is not substantial, most of these having gone off to Shanghai, but there are some. I noted in the card catalogue genealogies of the Fan family, the former owners of Tianyige, and a seventeenth-century edition of the Wan lineage—very important locally and nationally, the family of Wan Biao, Wan Sitong, etc.

We were told, I believe by Lü Zuoxie in Nanjing, that local teachers in Jinhua, Zhejiang, were collecting sources and interviewing with the intention of compiling a local history there.

A few publications picked up during the trip are worth noting. The Qingshi Yanjiusuo of Renmin University published a documentary history of Chengde, *Chengde bishu shanzhuang*, in August 1980. Their *Kang-Yong-Qian shiqi cheng xiang renmin fankang douzheng ziliao* [Documents on popular resistance movements in the Yongzheng and Qianlong reigns] (2 vols.), published in August 1979, is a catalogue of disturbances (arranged by place, time, and topic) described in the Qing archives and other collections. A collection of inscriptions from Beijing, *Ming-Qing yilai Beijing gongshang huiguan beike xuanbian* [Selected stone inscriptions of Beijing guilds in the Ming and Qing dynasties], by Li Hua, was published in June 1980. The collection was assembled in 1961. The author also collaborated in the Renmin University *Kang-Yong-Qian* work. The Tushu Ziliao Shi of the Shanghai Museum published a collection of inscriptions from around the municipality, *Shanghai beike ziliao xuanji* [Selected Shanghai stone inscriptions], in June 1980. In May 1980, the Shanghai Guji Chuban She published an early nineteenth-century record of the history of famous sites around Huqiu, just north of Suzhou, entitled *Tongqiao jizhuo lu*, by Gu Lu. Wu Guifang, of the Shanghai Museum, published the immensely popular *Gudai Shanghai shulüe* [Accounts of old Shanghai] in February 1980; the work was sold out when we reached Shanghai in early November. Copies are available in this country.

It seems appropriate to add that although interest in local history runs high among nonacademics, the obstacles to actually working on it remain formidable. With the single exception of Ye Xian'en, we met no one who had engaged in field work or worked analytically with documents in a local context—that is, no one who was doing the social or economic history of a place. Given the apparent lack of communication between academic historians and the local historian or antiquarian who takes pride in his native place, we are at a loss to see how local historical studies might develop.

One especially thorny problem involves the academic turf. Outside Beijing, the places we visited with the greatest concentration of researchers were Nanjing and Shanghai. The former is producing historians of Jiangsu province, and the latter is producing historians of Shanghai municipality. If current institutional structures continue to dominate, these historians will not apply their training elsewhere, nor will other centers send researchers to work on Jiangsu or Shanghai. Academic institutions outside Zhejiang province cannot send researchers there to develop the fertile field we observed, nor do Zhejiang historians study with their neighbors to the north. Talent, it seems, continues to be concentrated in central places, and localities beyond the institutional reach of this talent continue to guard their resources jealously.

What would the intrusion of American scholarship into this situation mean? Access remains a problem, even in Shanghai and Nanjing—our request to visit the Nanjing Library was denied, and all reports indicate that access to rare material in the Shanghai Library is limited at best. In Shaoxing, personal connections were not sufficient to get us a visit to the Lu Xun Memorial Library. And Chinese scholars report similar inability to gain access to sources in major libraries or to work outside their own turf—even in their native places—or to help foreign scholars to do so. These sorts of problems will not make senior American research scholars the friendliest of emissaries. On the other hand, non-Chinese who are willing to take the lumps may serve as catalysts in overcoming the turf problem or as models and sources of information on how local history is done in the West. Most of our group found it hard to be optimistic with regard to these problems.

STUDIES OF SONG HISTORY IN THE PEOPLE'S REPUBLIC

Brian E. McKnight

The majority of American scholars who have visited the People's Republic of China have either been specialists on Ming, Qing, or modern history, or on Han and pre-Han history. The visit of the Ming-Qing delegation was of especial value since the final report by Frederic Wakeman *et alia* serves as a good introduction not only to the state of Ming-Qing studies in China today but also to many of the archives and libraries of interest to scholars studying China. These visits have thus contributed to a better understanding of studies in China of the periods with which the Ming-Qing group was concerned. Until the Sino-American history symposium, historians studying the Song period had only a very imperfect picture of the extent and character of work being done in the People's Republic. This lack of information reflected both the difficulty of following historical debates and studies from outside China and, in part, the rapidly developing situation there with regard to historical studies.

During the symposium and the ensuing tour, it was possible to make contact with many Song specialists and gain invaluable information about current and prospective work in the field. The initial and most important contacts were made during the symposium itself. Four Chinese papers dealt with the Song. In addition, Zhou Baozhu, an assistant professor at Honan Normal University, gave the two American Song specialists copies of his paper, "The Economic Development of the Song Eastern Capital and Its Place in the Economic and Cultural Interchange of China and the Outside World" ("Songdai Dongjing chengshi jingjide fazhan ji chi zai Zhong-wai jingji wenhua jiaoliu zhongde diwei").

Discussions during the symposium and tour make possible a preliminary assessment of Song studies in the People's Republic. First, there is a recently founded, national umbrella organization of those interested in the Song, which at present has about seventy members. This group is headed by a five-man steering committee including Professor Deng Guangming of Beijing University, Professor Chen Lesu of Jinan University, and Professor Cheng Yingliu of Shanghai Normal College, who is the current director. The symposium enabled especially fruitful discussions since both Deng Guangming and Cheng Yingliu participated; Professor Deng delivered a paper on the economic impact of the professional army during the Northern Song, and Professor Cheng contributed a study of certain aspects of Song cities.

The newly founded Song organization plans to hold conferences on Song studies every other year. The first such conference was held in October 1980 in Shanghai. In all there were forty-one papers covering a wide variety of topics, from the philosophy of Ju Xi to the Song system of land tenure. Roughly a quarter of the papers dealt specifically with the economy, with such topics as the Song system of merchant taxes, the system of land sales, various aspects of trade, the land tax system, and some questions concerning monetary developments. Another substantial group of essays dealt with such social issues as the status of guest households (kehu), middle-ranking households in the villages, and "official households" (guanhu); the system of village population registration; clan organizations; and Song cities. A third group of papers covered military developments. Finally, there were two papers on law and several that dealt with individual figures or with specific historical texts. There were no papers on the arts or letters.

In addition to the paper presentations, the October Shanghai meeting also included small group discussions of particular problems raised by some of the papers. The discussions were spirited and revealed substantial differences of viewpoint on some central themes of Song history, e.g., whether Song economic development resulted in a relative "loosening" of status in rural areas or in a greater degree of control over rural people. Such discussions are heartening insofar as they indicate the potential vitality of Song studies. Unfortunately, they also reflect how isolated the historians in China have been, since the issues appear to be largely repetitions of similar debates among Japanese historians for the past fifty years. This in turn suggests that current moves to increase foreign-language skills, particularly Japanese for historical studies and English for theoretical work, will aid future development of the field.

At the Shanghai meeting, the importance of considering regional variations in development and of studying continuities with pre- and post-Song eras was stressed. The delegates also indicated their support for defining "Song" studies broadly so as to encompass the study of contemporary states such as Xixia, Liao, and Jin.

Some of the conference delegates visited Shanghai Normal College, where they conferred with the group directed by Professor Cheng Yingliu which is currently punctuating the important annalistic history of the Northern Song, the Xu zizhi tongjian changbian. Volumes two through eight are now in print. The first volume will be a mulu (index) and will appear after the other volumes have been issued. The group hoped to complete the project of punctuating the Changbian in 1981 and intended then to turn to punctuating the Wenxian tongkao.

The Shanghai meeting also resolved to seek continuing publication of their newsletter. One number of this newsletter was issued prior to the Shanghai conference, and several more appeared during the proceedings. It will presumably continue as an irregular publication. A decision was also made to compile a bibliography of works on the Song by scholars outside of China. I am corresponding with members of the steering committee concerning bibliographies of Japanese and Western works on the period. This is one example of another stated goal of the members of the Chinese Song group, that of establishing closer ties with foreign scholars. Finally, the group resolved to seek increased publication of Song source materials and scholarship.

In addition to this national organization, another mechanism for encouraging Song studies in the People's Republic has been the establishment of (unrelated) study groups at various academic and research centers. Such groups exist at Honan Normal University (where the group is headed by Professor Zhang Bingren, with Assistant Professor Zhou Baozhu serving as assistant director); at Hangzhou University (with Professor Xu Gui as director and Assistant Professor Liang Taiji as assistant director); and at the National Academy of Social Sciences (Beijing), Historical Research Section (headed by Li Jiaju). These groups are generally simply Song study groups, but the group at the Academy of Social Sciences is called the Song-Liao-Jin-Yuan study group, and the one at Beijing University is a Tang-Song study group.

Without a thorough examination of all of the papers delivered at the Shanghai meeting, it is not possible to speak with complete confidence about the quality of Song studies in China. However, judging from the materials that are available it does seem clear that the difficulties of the past decades and the isolation of Chinese scholars have prevented them from making the kinds of contributions that might otherwise have been possible. Many of the questions now being raised are significant, but Chinese historians have not been in a position to make use of the considerable Japanese scholarship on Song China, nor have their approaches been affected by developments, Marxist or non-Marxist, in the Western social sciences. The founding of the national Song society and the activities of the local study groups, unrelated to the national society, are very hopeful signs that Chinese historians will in the future have the interest and, under the current, more open situation, the opportunity to make great progress in Song studies. It is particularly important that they do so. Although it is still true that American students interested in the Song should do the bulk of their research abroad in Japan, it is also true that interest in Song studies in Japan is on the wane. The older Song scholars there are not being replaced. Only in the People's Republic is there a body of Song scholars large enough both to undertake new and varied kinds of research on the Song and to maintain a high level of interest in the period.

The Song papers delivered at the Beijing symposium suggested one important area of potentially fruitful cooperation between Chinese and American specialists—the study of urban history. Of the five Song papers we received, three focused on urban history. For Song specialists the topic is a natural one. During the Song, Chinese cities were the largest and most highly developed urban concentrations in the world. Moreover, the topic is one which has attracted Chinese and foreign scholars studying later dynasties. Despite this interest, and despite a great variety of source material as yet not fully exploited, urban historical studies of China are less sophisticated than those of Europe or the United States. Again, the isolation of Chinese scholars and the impact of the troubles of recent decades have hindered the development of the field. In any cooperative investigation of Chinese urban history, American scholars will be able to share with their Chinese colleagues the methodological and theoretical sophistication developed by Western geographers, sociologists, historians, and economists. Although leading figures in the field, e.g., Brian Berry, have now moved sharply away from the earlier emphasis on development of central-place theory and the field is now in a state of flux, the Chinese would no doubt benefit from an awareness of the kinds of questions raised by urban geographers, by the Urban History Group at Leicester, England, or in the pages of the *Urban Anthropology Newsletter, The Journal of Urban History*, or the *Urban History Group Newsletter* in the United States. While the Chinese might gain from this introduction to methodological and theoretical work, the Western participants would certainly benefit from superior Chinese control of access to printed and manuscript sources. Furthermore, only in China is there the quantity of historians to make feasible the investigation of many important questions. Finally, the topic of urban history also has the advantage of side-stepping the landlord-tenant question which dominates much Chinese historical research.

Scholars from outside China could bring to such cooperation not only methodological expertise but also substantive knowledge. Shiba Yoshinobu and his associates have spent a number of years studying the city of Ningbo and its hinterland. Although plans for a multidisciplinary study of the region have now been abandoned, the pattern used, that of studying urban-rural relations and integrating economic and social analysis, could form a profitable avenue for future studies.

In researching a study of Hangzhou, I am currently corresponding with Song historians who have worked on urban history to explore the possibility of cooperative studies of urban history. As a first step, I am trying to locate Chinese historians studying the Song through the Qing who have worked on urban history. A list of such scholars would be useful since Chinese historians are usually organized either in terms of time periods or according to historical problems (such as the Taiping Rebellion). If a core group can be established, it might then be possible to establish certain common questions and approaches, even before joint projects could be undertaken. If the Chinese are interested in pursuing cooperative projects, it may be worthwhile to hold a small gathering of Chinese and American scholars to discuss possible projects.

DEMOGRAPHIC VARIABLES IN CHINESE HISTORY:
A PERCEIVED CHALLENGE TO THE THEORY OF CLASS STRUGGLE

Gilbert Rozman

During the course of his summary at the symposium's concluding session, Yan Zhongping injected one qualification into his generally positive evaluation. Reviewing the broad range of topics discussed, Yan argued that it is necessary to find an axis that will link them together—much as a Beijing local delicacy resembling shishkebob is skewered on a stick. Not surprisingly, he proclaimed that axis to be the social class interpretation of history. Challenging the American participants to conduct their own search, Yan specifically singled out the subject of population as an unworthy contender. After all, he observed with somewhat strained logic, how could population variables account for peasant uprisings—situations in which poverty incites large numbers of people, but obviously not aristocrats, to act? Nor, he insisted, could long-term low productivity per worker, associated during the course of the conference with high population densities, explain the short-term incidence of uprisings. Yan was not alone in this critical reaction to the efforts by me and, from time to time, other Americans to emphasize population variables. A number of Chinese expressed themselves on this matter and in so doing generally reaffirmed their acceptance of a form of class analysis that they seemed to find difficult to reconcile with demographically oriented interpretations.

Ambivalence in the Chinese response to the American papers was especially evident in the area of population studies—one of the primary arenas of recent advances in historical scholarship outside of China. On the one hand, the Chinese participants accepted the desirability of many unfamiliar ways of looking at their history, for example, the systematic application of quantitative methods, the emphasis on explicit comparisons with other premodern societies, and the detailed attention to the international impact on the premodern economy. Some of their more positive responses occurred in the formal and informal discussion of population variables. On the other hand, there was considerable vigor in the defensive reaffirmation of long-standing assumptions about social class. I found it regrettable that at times the mood of this reaffirmation was less one of mutual interest in improved sources, methods, and topics to test the validity of differing interpretations than one of confrontation based on unquestioned assumptions.

The Contemporary Background

Along Chang'an Jie, the main thoroughfare of Beijing, a prominent sign advises that bearing only one child is best *(sheng yige hao)*. In recent months the newspapers of China have featured countless articles on the critical consequences of China's large population and its rate of growth vis-à-vis modern development. Only several years ago it was class struggle that was considered decisive in determining China's future development. It would not seem to require much ingenuity for historians (if not inclined to make a similar abrupt transformation) at least to seek the roots of the current population dilemma and to inquire about corresponding consequences in other periods of social change. Were scholars to decide the matter, it would be difficult to imagine more ideal circumstances for challenging the exclusive preoccupation with class struggle in history.

In 1980, articles on demographic history in certain dynasties began to appear, but, it seems, they were without general interpretations of the impact of demography on social change. None of the Chinese papers distributed for the symposium treated the historical population with more than a passing reference. Despite the fiction that what matters before the socialist revolution is virtually distinct from what matters in its aftermath, I suspect that the salience of contemporary population considerations has created some interest in attempts to draw the attention of historians to this subject.

The Clash of Interpretations

Chen Zhenhan, an economist from Beijing University, singled out for discussion one provocative sentence in my paper on "Historical Demography: Sources and Indicators for the Study of the Qing Population."

> It would perhaps not be much of an exaggeration to claim that in certain circles the expectations that once focused on reinterpreting China's past in terms of class conflict are now centered on population and related variables with due consideration to regional and local variations as well as to urban-rural and social class differences—a reinterpretation of social history with parallels in recent research on the impact of population growth for modernization.

Chen insisted that no Chinese are in these circles. He then offered a definitive division of interpretations of history in terms of two categories: (1) ultimate causality exemplified by the Marxist theory of class struggle and (2) functional relations involving such variables as population which, although they do not constitute the base of history, must be taken into account. In this manner, he relegated my paper and the other American papers to second-class status. Although that is far better than having no status at all, this perspective to some extent detracted from serious consideration of the contents of our papers.

The explicit or implicit classification of scholarship into two categories persisted throughout the conference. At the second substantive session on Monday afternoon, Evelyn Rawski's emphasis on literacy rates (a measure that incorporates population data) aroused the most impassioned discussion. The rebuttal stressed that what really matters is the class-based moral content of education. The Chinese educational system was described as a barrier to both economic and scientific development—a viewpoint which, in essence, dispenses with the need for any inquiry into its per capita distribution. A similar point came up in the discussion of my paper. It was argued, correctly, that such indicators as mean household size cannot fully reflect the complexity of local social and economic conditions; therefore, population studies by themselves are insufficient. Yet, it was my strong impression that the point being made was not simply that one cannot get an accurate overview from data from certain periods, from certain localities, and pertinent to certain indicators, with which no one would argue, but also that inherent in any work on variables such as population was a narrow approach which could not realize substantial advances without being linked to a social class interpretation of history.

Demography was not the only topic that was perceived as a challenge to class struggle explanations. Fu-mei Chen's analysis of landlord-tenant relationships, which stressed the contractual equality of the two parties and the protection offered by the prevalence of permanent tenancy, produced one of the most direct challenges to Chinese interpretations of exploitation. Again, the criticisms concerned both the representativeness of the findings and the absence of an overview on landlord-tenant relationships. Albert Feuerwerker's paper on the state's limited role in the economy was seen as another direct challenge to a class viewpoint. Deng Guangming responded that the negative impact on economic development of the state's harsh policies in controlling the peasants had been underestimated.

Late in the conference, papers by G. William Skinner and Robert Hartwell, both of which incorporated population growth and density as major factors in their regional approaches, were criticized for pretensions of comprehensiveness and neglect of crucial variables. In the same vein, Yeh-chien Wang's study of grain prices and William Atwell's periodization based on the flow of silver were regarded as incomplete without class analysis. Indeed, at least two Chinese papers, Wang Yuquan's innovative reinterpretation of peasant status and Guo Songyi's examination of state reclamation policies, became targets of criticism from other Chinese for their omission or neglect of landowner exploitation and class struggle. To some degree (but, I must emphasize, within limits that allowed a fruitful discussion to proceed), the criticism of papers for their failure to treat "ultimate causality" interfered with a full assessment on other grounds.

In my paper I referred briefly to attempts outside of China to treat population as an explanatory variable, e.g., for administrative deterioration, relative technological stagnation, and peasant rebellions. A number of American criticisms of Chinese papers pointed to the neglect of this variable in their efforts to explain various types of social change. On Monday morning both Feuerwerker and I found Li Wenzhi's interpretation of why "sprouts of capitalism" in agriculture failed to grow deficient due to its omission of how population growth might have interfered with the accumulation of a surplus. Comments on Chen Zhen's study of Kaifeng in the Song period noted its weak use of urban population statistics. The issue of urbanization resurfaced in Feuerwerker's paper and in objections to his claim to have demonstrated that premodern China in the accumulation of a surplus was close to an upper limit shared with European countries. I argued that a sharp rise in urbanization occurred in England, France, Russia, and Japan, but not in China, and that it is important to focus on why China did not draw more rural resources into cities. In another instance of Americans criticizing each other's work (a phenomenon that prompted Deng Guangming, serving as moderator, to remark that our sessions were becoming more and more lively as Chinese criticized Chinese, American criticized American, and the two sides criticized each other), Yeh-chien Wang also argued that China's low tax rates kept it well away from any possible upper limit, and Skinner suggested that per capita growth is characteristic of the upswing in regional cycles. While the Americans disagreed on how to make use of comparative population and urban data, the Chinese often failed even to express burdens in per capita terms, e.g., citing evidence for increasing absolute amounts of tax without considering the impact of population growth on the per capita rate. The Chinese papers also evidenced serious errors in the use of population statistics on occasion. In my commentary on Wang Sizhi's paper, I questioned his statement that the population of China tripled during the sixty years of the Qianlong reign, noting that the early records from this reign are not true population counts. It is, of course, understandable that roughly thirty years of virtual isolation from scholarship abroad complicates the research of Chinese historians. In short, the class struggle perspective mainly entered papers through misconceived questions and unquestioned assumptions which discussants asked the Chinese authors to reconsider by taking into account other possible explanatory variables; and population was largely neglected or carelessly treated, which led to suggestions for incorporating that subject more systematically. Chinese scholars, both publicly and privately, seemed to welcome those suggestions.

The Search for Better Sources and Methods

For the most part, our search for superior primary sources and empirical data and our methods of analyzing the data elicited a favorable reaction. At the same time, the Chinese quickly became aware that we responded most positively to their empirical research, e.g., the praise given to Cong Hanxiang's use of more than 250 gazetteers for studying the distribution of cotton production. Each side complimented the other's use of new or previously un-derutilized sources. By implication we were also passing judgment on the distressingly narrow range of primary sources available to the Chinese on most of the subjects they studied. They were apologizing, without assigning blame, for not having read more widely in secondary sources, while we hoped that not only would they begin to read the international scholarship but that they would also increasingly take advantage of their superior language skills and archival resources by utilizing new primary sources.

With regard to population sources, the response of Chinese discussants and archivists was not all that we might have hoped for. Yet, the new information divulged also proved of considerable importance. Chen Zhenhan, citing his suspicions of the feudal state, expressed doubts that government sources would prove very helpful, but he did encourage research on *jiapu* (genealogies) and estimated that 10 to 20 percent of the more than 100,000 *jiapu* extant in the 1950s have survived. Peng Zeyi praised the source on Tianjin that I had used and the value of utilizing sources other than *fangzhi* (local gazetteers). I later privately took partial exception to his remark that *fangzhi* do not permit calcu-lation of the percentage of the population in cities.

The major commentary on sources came from Ju Deyuan, the responsible person at the Ming-Qing archive in Beijing. Ju suggested that we foreigners are at fault for only paying attention to published government sources and knowing so little of the abundance of population records that can be found in China's archives. He insisted that we (nothing was said about the Chinese themselves) need to put in more time at the archives. Ju listed sources with relatively complete and systematic records: (1) 8,200 volumes (called *yudie*) on the imperial banners giving dates of birth, death, and marriage; (2) detailed records kept by the Libu on virtuous women; (3) midwife *(shoushengpo)* certificates; and (4) population reports *(hukouce)* covering banner estate lands. Ju claimed that the variables I had indicated were difficult to measure—fertility, mortality, nuptiality—can be determined from these sources. While these remarks did not encourage us to expect collaborative undertakings or independent Chinese research, the new information was certainly exciting coming only six days before Ju was scheduled to show us his archive and I was to begin one week of research there on population sources.

The visit to the Ming-Qing archive was of great interest. The then director, Huang Xiaozeng, mentioned that archival work had resumed in April (by which, we gathered, he meant that the archive had been placed under new authority; in December 1979 I had worked in the archive for two days and other Americans had begun using them earlier) and that the goal was to serve research on history. Because work had only recently resumed, he apologized, all of our requests might not be fulfilled. The tour of the inner areas of the archive gave us a chance to see some of the population records mentioned at the conference. However, we could not see the catalogues (some Americans had previously been shown them), and we were told that there are many materials (including all maps) that foreigners are not allowed to see. Our group was allowed to examine more closely only the materials set aside for us in advance, and while doing so, most of the group could not take notes. Only Yeh-chien Wang and I were exempted from this last limitation because we had received prior permission to stay over in Beijing to use these materials.

After one week's examination of a few examples (all late Qing) of the *yudie* and the *hukouce*, I found that a few *yudie* by themselves were inadequate for serious research. I am not in a position to make a general assessment, but the coverage of deaths and living young children seems sporadic. If many more volumes indeed exist and if they offer a continuous record over much of the Qing period, the omissions may not be so serious. This has potential for constructing a life table for males above a certain age.

My own research centered on the *hukouce*, and I was surprised to find out that only three exist (one is too damaged for me to be allowed to use it), each dating from about 1905. I had time to record the ages for the residents of nine villages, a sample of 3,646 persons. I began the analysis of age distributions and sex ratios and found the data for males above age fifteen and females above age twenty of potential value. I did not have time to copy down family relationships for more than a small fraction of the population and would urge that a full copy of these records be obtained for future research. I was not allowed to see enough sources to obtain a general impression about Ju's claims for the value of these sources.

I found satisfaction in: (1) at last having the opportunity, along with others, to communicate with PRC scholars who are clearly interested in improving the quality of scholarship on Chinese history; (2) striving to speed the incorporation of population variables into historical studies as part of the reorientation of research that is under way in China; (3) learning of unknown archival sources; and (4) conducting one week's research on some of these previously unknown sources, which have utility for understanding China's population history. Population studies is an area where the potential for collaboration is high; it can serve as a measure of how fast the barriers to both improved research and international collaboration come down.

STUDIES OF LEGAL HISTORY AND OTHER OBSERVATIONS

Fu-mei Chang Chen

The Sino-American history symposium brought together a range of scholars, including well-known, established historians such as Wang Yuquan, Wei Qingyuan, Li Wenzhi, and Peng Zeyi; but, significantly, a younger contingent generated discussion of new and very promising work on many different aspects of Chinese social and economic history. I discovered that Li Min, who did an excellent study on the "sprouts of capitalism" in agriculture as found in routine memorials during the Qianlong reign (see *Wenwu*, 1975), was the pen name used by Liu Yongcheng, an associate research fellow at the Institute of History, CASS. Similarly, Ouyang Fanxiu, another scholar who has worked extensively on the legal status of hired laborers during the Qing dynasty, turned out to be Jing Junjian, who holds the same position in the Academy's Institute of Economics. I especially enjoyed meeting two female participants, Cong Hanxiang and Han Hengyu; the latter's interest in Qing servile relationships closely parallels my own.

One accomplishment of the symposium was to bring together a number of younger scholars who live outside of Beijing. They are mostly in their early forties and have great potential. Yang Guozhen and Lin Renchuan of Xiamen University in Fujian, Ye Xian'en of Zhongshan University in Guangdong, Bao Yanbang of Jinan University in Guangzhou, and Ran Guangrong of Sichuan University, to name just a few, were impressive for their competence in their chosen specialties. These young scholars would have much to contribute to our research if exchange arrangements can facilitate further contact.

Since I was born and educated in Taiwan, I became quite popular among the Chinese historians. They are basically shy with foreigners, but I was considered at least "half-Chinese and half-American." In many of our private conversations we were able to exchange views rather freely. They were most interested in what Chinese scholars on Taiwan are doing and wanted to know about the major publications of the last thirty years. Only one or two of them had been able to buy books published in Taiwan. The budget in various universities and institutions is very tight; after appropriations for books dealing with science and technology have been made, there is little money left for history or other social science books. Books published in Taiwan are attractive for two reasons: they tend to be cheap and are easier to use than books in foreign languages. I promised to send catalogues from a few major publishing houses in Taibei so that Chinese scholars would have some idea about what is available there. They are eager to work out some kind of exchange program with American institutions. Obviously, a third party in Hong Kong or Singapore will be needed to facilitate the transshipment since it is not yet possible to mail books directly from Taiwan to the PRC.

Because I have been interested in studying and collecting land deeds and other legal documents, I took careful notes whenever I got a chance to examine such documents in archives in Beijing and elsewhere. I also tried to familiarize myself with recent developments in the field of Chinese legal history.

In the first decade after the founding of the People's Republic, Chinese jurists looked to the Soviet model to establish China's socialist legality. They did not pay much attention to their own legal heritage. The only exception is an excellent annotated work on the Legal Treatise from the Qing Draft History, called *Qingshigao xingfazhi zhujie*, produced in 1957 by four members of the Legal History Research Division, Bureau of Legal Affairs, State Council. This is probably the only work that can be viewed as a major contribution to the field of Chinese legal history.

Professor Qu Tongzu is a well-known scholar in that field. In the early 1960s he returned to China from the United States. His arrival, however, did not seem to have any visible impact. For various reasons he simply stopped producing; nor is there any indication that he guided his students to publish scholarly work. The field remained dormant for many years. Indeed, for the first twenty-five years of the PRC, it would be difficult to put together a respectable volume on the history of Chinese law, either narrowly or broadly defined, by combing through journals and newspaper articles throughout the entire country. Law was considered insignificant, for one of the goals of the new China was to achieve a society that could dispense with law. That being the case, the history of traditional law was certainly more dispensible than the living law.

In the post-Cultural Revolution era, the government emphasized the role of law and reasserted its desire to establish socialist legality. A new interest in China's legal heritage began to emerge. *Faxue yanjiu* [Studies in law] made its debut in 1978, and *Minzhu yu fazhi* [Democracy and legality] commenced publication a year later. *Renmin sifa* [People's judiciary], *Renmin jiancha* [People's procuracy], and *Renmin gongan* [People's public security] all tried to heighten the citizens' awareness of the "rule of law." A substantial number of articles dealing with China's legal heritage can be found in these magazines. The topics cover a wide range: they might be as specific as a commentary on a noted criminal case in antiquity or as general as a discussion of the overall features of the traditional Chinese legal system that set itself apart from the rest of the world. The time frame might range from antiquity to the Yan'an period. Books also began to appear. One useful volume is *Zhongguo gudai ban'an baili* [One hundred annotated ancient judicial cases] (1980), compiled by a team of seven scholars from the Legal History Research Division, Institute of Law, CASS. They selected, annotated, and translated into *baihua* more than a hundred short entries (most of them anecdotes) from dynastic histories and miscellaneous essays to show that the "rule of law" is part of the Chinese tradition. Another book worth noting is *Zhongguo xianfa shilüe* [A brief account of the history of Chinese constitutions] by Zhang Jinfan and Zeng Xianyi which includes materials from the Republican period. Every now and then we find good articles in journals and newspapers. The discovery of Qin bamboo strips in the late 1975 excavation in Yunmen county, Hubei province, prompted several scholars to study Qin law. Their findings have been published primarily in *Wenwu*, but occasionally articles crop up in other publications (e.g., *Shehui kexue zhanxian* [Social science ideological front], January 1979).

The revived interest in traditional law culminated in a Symposium on Chinese Legal History and the History of Chinese Legal Thought, which took place from 12 to 18 September 1979 in Changchun. More than eighty law teachers, jurists, and publishers of legal materials met to exchange views and discuss future plans. At the symposium, Mr. Sun Yeming, director of the Institute of Law, CASS, delivered the keynote speech, in which he reaffirmed the contribution made by ancient Chinese law to the development of world civilization. He also stressed the need to engage in the study of the traditional judicial system as well as the evolution of Chinese legal thought. The outcome of such study might be helpful not only in adopting new legislation but also in current law enforcement and the enrichment of legal theories. An Association for the History of Chinese Law (Zhongguo Falüshi Xuehui) was formally established at the symposium. A charter was adopted and the key personnel of the new organization elected. (A brief account of this symposium appears in *Guangming ribao*, 2 October 1979.)

Participants at the symposium agreed to undertake the task of producing two multivolume compendia. One is called *Chinese Legal History (Zhongguo fazhishi)*, with Xie Tieguang of the Institute of Law, CASS, as chief editor; and the other is the *History of Chinese Legal Thought (Zhongguo falü sixiangshi)*, with Li Guangcan in charge. Apparently, Gao Min is working on Qin law, Gao Heng on the Han period, Yang Tingfu of Shanghai Normal University on the Tang, and Zhang Jinfan of People's University in Beijing on Qing law.

During our sojourn in Beijing, I did not get a chance to meet any scholar who specialized in the study of Chinese legal history. When we started our journey to the south, it occurred to me that I should try to meet someone in the field. The day after we arrived in Shanghai I made a special request to see

Professor Yang Tingfu, who had participated in the Changchun symposium. Though it was very short notice, Tang Zhijun of the Shanghai Municipal Academy of Social Sciences went out of his way to accommodate my wishes. The following day I had a long and fruitful conversation with Professor Yang. Professor Brian McKnight of our delegation sat in on the meeting.

The following account is drawn from my notes of our visits to various archives and university libraries.

Number One Archive, Beijing

Director Huang Xiaozeng gave some brief introductory comments. Deputy Chief Ju Deyuan showed us some samples. I was most interested in the *zhupi falülei*, legal documents endorsed by Qing emperors from Kangxi to Xuantung (serial nos. 1-194). An initial classification and arrangement of these items had been completed.

Mr. Ju then led us to the storage rooms for a guided tour. Most of the files from the Board of Punishments were kept on level four, upstairs. These are the so-called *xingbu hongben*, which contain a complete record of cases deliberated by members of the Board. The entries were classified according to the nature of the offense. Sometimes the original findings made by district magistrates were also included. These are very rich primary source materials heretofore untouched by scholars. It would be a legal historian's paradise if they could be removed for an in-depth analysis. Apparently, in 1979 members of the Ming-Qing delegation were able to see a rough catalogue of the entire collection that had been prepared in the 1930s. We asked for a catalogue but were not allowed to see one.

After the guided tour we were shown some samples that we had requested a few days earlier. I was permitted to examine two sets of materials closely. The first set was comprised of *xingke tiben*—eight routine memorials handled by the censorate's Section of Punishments, dating from the ninth month of Qianlong 32 (1767). All of the entries are related to capital offenses—the offenders' names were ready to be checked off for execution. A few of the documents contain detailed deliberations on the crime and the proposed sentence. The emperor's final decision is also recorded. A careful study of such documents will shed much light on the death penalty in Qing China. All eight documents are written in both Chinese and Manchu. The second set were *zhupi zouzhe, falülei, shenpan* from Jiaqing 6-8 (1801-1803). Several cases are related to a citizen's making a direct appeal in the nation's capital (Jingkong). The documents are written in Chinese only.

Beijing Historical Museum

A group of scholars are at work on Ming and Qing land deeds, rent books, and fish-scale registers. There are about 3,000 items all together. Each item is placed in a brown envelope, given a simple notation by a researcher, and then endorsed by Wang Hongjun. I saw one land contract dated Hongwu 6 (1373); it was quite similar to late Qing contracts I have studied elsewhere. The only major difference I detected is that the sale price was paid in cotton cloth rather than in silver or copper cash. Mr. Wang told me that the group intended to publish these materials in the future. We were not allowed to copy anything.

Number Two Archive, Nanjing

Director Tang Biao received our delegation warmly and offered some introductory remarks. The holdings include government and miscellaneous materials from 1912 to 1949, from both the Beiyang and Guomindang periods. There are some 910,000 files *(juanhao)*. Each file contains one or more entries.

Soon after Liberation, the central government decided to begin collecting these materials. Originally, the ones from the Beiyang government were located primarily in the north. In the 1948-1949 period, as the Guomindang regime fled Nanjing, it attempted to take along a large number of government documents. Crate after crate of important documents were dropped along the escape route to Taiwan. The Communists simply retrieved the discarded ones. There is no inventory of the items that were taken to Taiwan. Through planning and hard work, all of the scattered materials have finally been gathered together and given a permanent home here.

The holdings are arranged in two ways. The *guiyuan* system assigns each document to the government branch where it originated. The document is then classified in accordance with the jurisdiction in a particular department or section of that branch. The second system classifies documents according to their condition and topic. The first method is the more frequently used.

The Number Two Archive holds a complete set of the Nationalist government gazette. The gazettes published by the Judicial Yuan and the Legislative Yuan are incomplete. I told the archivists that the East Asian Collection of Hoover Institution at Stanford has been gathering *gongbao* publications. Perhaps by pooling together American and Chinese resources we can find the missing links. Upon my return to the United States, the curator of the EAC mailed a copy of Julia Tung's *Bibliography of Chinese Government Serials, 1880-1949, Material in Hoover Institution on War, Revolution and Peace* to Director Tang as a gift.

An Australian scholar working on the Beiyang government was able to spend two days at the archive. He will be permitted to return in the near future. American scholars have not yet been granted the same kind of access to these sources. (Since our visit to China, the Number Two Archive has been opened to foreign scholars to a greater degree.)

A group of scholars writing the history of the Republic of China, headed by Li Xin of the Institute of Modern History, has utilized the holdings of the archive extensively. So have the members of the Institute of Economics of the People's Bank in Beijing, who have recently compiled a book on the history of the Farmer's Bank in China. In addition, the Chinese Communist Party, in the process of compiling its party history, has also made use of the source materials housed in the Number Two Archive.

The archive is preparing two series of books which make available some of its rare and heretofore inaccessible documents. The first series is entitled Zhonghua Minguo Shi Dang'an Ziliao Huibian [A collection of archival materials on the history of the Republic of China]; its volumes give the 1912-1949 period a topical treatment. The first volume of the series is *Xinhai geming* [The 1911 revolution]. The second volume is entitled *Nanjing linshi zhengfu* [The Nanking provisional government]. The third volume will deal with Yuan Shikai. Publication of volumes in the series will continue until the year 1949 is reached. The second series is known as Zhonghua Minguo Shi Dang'an Ziliao Congkan. A volume entitled *Wusi yundong* [The May Fourth movement] is already available. More monographs are being readied for publication.

Nanjing University

We were permitted, on request, to see or copy any books or documents in this collection. The university gave each of us a copy of their rare-book catalogue, entitled *Nanjing daxue tushuguan cang, Guji shanben tushu mulu*.

A large number of Ming-Qing documents from Tunxi in Anhui province are kept in the library. It is by far the most valuable collection of its kind I have ever seen. It consists of a broad range of property transaction records as well as official documents like yellow registers, fish-scale registers, and depositions by criminal offenders. A few American scholars (among them Mi Chu Wiens and Kang Chao) have used some of these materials in recent years. Apparently, the Economics Institute of the Academy of Social Sciences in Beijing holds comparable materials from the same region and the same period, though not as numerous. In Taiwan, I believe, the late Professor Fang Hao had in his personal collection a batch of materials from the Ming and Qing originating from the same area. (Professor Fang had published a series of articles on his collection in *Shihuo Monthly*.) An attempt ought somehow to be made to pool together all three of these collections, but much work remains to be done in Nanjing first.

All of the Tunxi materials have been catalogued in a rudimentary fashion. I randomly picked up file no. 66. It has 230 red and white deeds from the Ming dynasty. An index card provides a detailed breakdown of the number of documents from each reign period. I examined five contracts from the Hongwu emperor's reign very carefully. They are in perfect condition. This is unquestionably a gold mine for legal historians.

Shanghai Library

This is the second largest library in China (next to the Beijing Library). It houses some 7 million books, among them 1.5 million *guji* (old books). A national directory of rare books, of which this library holds 150,000 volumes, is being prepared for publication in Beijing.

We were shown a few samples of rare books. The one I perused was called *Xin'an gucheng Chengshi lidai zongpu*, a Ming-edition genealogical record of the Cheng family of Xiuning, Anhui province, with a preface dated Longqing 2 (1568).

Shanghai Museum

During the Cultural Revolution, a number of Qing land deeds surfaced and were sent here. The exact number and the place of origin of these documents are unknown. They were roughly classified and placed in brown bags. I examined eight or nine documents, most of them from the nineteenth century.

Zhejiang Provincial Library, Hangzhou

This library is divided between two locations. Old books are housed in the outer West Lake, and new and foreign books are kept at the site on University Road. We visited the former only.

There are over 2 million old books; 6,000 of these are classified as rare ones. The library collects some manuscripts and hand-copied works. *Shougao* are an author's own manuscripts, *gaoben* are copies by his children, *chaoben* by his friends, and *chuanchaoben* by someone outside of these categories. A catalogue entitled *Guancang gaoben mulu* has been compiled by the library, but we did not get to see it.

In 1979 a small group of Japanese scholars visited this library and was permitted to use its materials.

Tianyige Library, Ningbo, Zhejiang

Built in 1561-1566 by a Ming Board of War official named Fan Qing, this is the oldest surviving repository of books in China (the original collection is intact). In 1940 a two-volume catalogue of rare books was published. There is currently a complete catalogue of rare books. For the rest of the collection, only a card catalogue exists. We were the first Americans to visit this library.

I asked to see three Ming law books. All of them are listed in the 1940 catalogue mentioned above. The first one, called Chongzeng shiyi daminglü, in seven juan, was out for repair and binding. The second one, called Daminglü, is in two ce from the Jiajing reign (1522-1566). Only the second volume survives. It looks like an official publication of the Ming legal code rather than a private edition. I copied a few of the small interlinear commentaries to the code. The third, Jiajing xinli, is a hand-copied work in one volume. It is a compilation of substatutes issued during the Jiajing period. At the end of each provision there is a brief account of the legislative history explaining what prompted the promulgation of that particular substatute.

Other samples were brought out for inspection. Some of them are very fragile. Judging by the date of the newspapers that were used in wrapping books, it appears that some of the volumes that we examined had not been opened since 1935 or so.

NOTES ON THE SPROUTS OF CAPITALISM

Yeh-chien Wang

The scholarly discussions on the sprouts of capitalism (or incipient capitalism) continue unabated in the People's Republic of China today. To the Chinese academic community the term means the development of China's premodern economy in the late imperial period, approximately from 1500 to 1840, in which the spread of the country's commodity economy accelerated and led to the emergence of a new (capitalist) mode of production. The capitalist mode of production is a productive system consisting of the capitalist and free wage earners in which the former hires the latter on a contract basis to produce commodities for sale and to make a profit. Three papers at the symposium dealt with this significant issue; more appear in various journals. In this short essay I present some of the recent contributions to this discussion based on what I learned on this trip.

The Role of the State

In the historiography of the People's Republic, the state prior to 1949 is cast as a villain, preserving tenaciously the vested interests of the ruling class of landlords and suppressing any demand for social and economic changes from other social classes. In a paper on the development of handicraft industries in the early Qing, Peng Zeyi introduces what appears to be a rather unorthodox view. He maintains that the state played a positive role in increasing productivity (thereby promoting social and economic development) because various restrictions previously imposed upon artisans and handicraft industries were relaxed in order to revive the war-torn economy following more than a half-century of civil strife. Foremost among the liberalizing policies adopted by the early Manchu government was the abolition of the system of artisan registration. In the Ming dynasty all artisans were registered as a separate class and their status was hereditary. They had to work without compensation for the state for a certain period of time each year. In 1645 the Qing government abolished the system and freed artisans from a subjected status. This resulted, Peng believes, in raising their incentive in productive activities.

51

Moreover, the Qing government converted most taxes that were previously paid in kind into cash payment. The conversion of taxes had the effect of broadening the market for handicraft products. For not only did peasants have to sell a greater part of the goods they produced (grain, cotton cloth, silk rolls, etc.) in order to meet their tax obligations, but it also became necessary for the government to purchase from the market what it used to collect by way of taxation. In addition, the government scaled down the size and operation of public enterprises such as silk and porcelain factories and removed some regulatory strictures against private mining industry. These policies provided further stimuli to the market economy and fostered the growth of productivity.

We find some support for Peng's view in another paper read by Li Wenzhi at the symposium. Li thinks that the Manchu government helped promote the sprouts of capitalism in the agricultural sector. Before 1768, he states, there was no legal equality between the landlord and the agricultural worker hired on a long-term contract. The relationship between them was that of master and servant. The revised code stipulated, however, that employer (should he be a commoner landlord) and the worker he hired should "sit and eat together" and that they should "call each other on the basis of equality." The change in legal status was, in Li's view, conducive to the development of the kind of employer-employee relationship that is free from servitude. And he notes that on the basis of the archival material on penal laws he has investigated thus far, the percentage of agricultural workers on a long-term contract who were still subject to servitude after 1768 was very small.

Market Demand

Following the Marxist interpretation, Chinese historians have stressed the advance of social productive force or the rise of productivity as the prerequisite to changes in the mode of production. There are, however, some indications that certain scholars are turning their attention to demand-side economics and trying to present a more balanced view—one which sees the "sprouts" as a result of the interplay between rising productivity and an expanding market. Again, we may look to Peng's paper on this point. While laboring hard to prove the increase in productivity in the early Qing, Peng points to the significant contribution from the increase in market demand.[1] The fact that the market was growing in the early Qing, he says, can be attributed to the growth of population, the establishment of new prefectures and districts, the development

---

[1] In most cases, what Peng and other historians in the PRC mean by the increase of productivity is simply an increase in production, not necessarily a rise in per capita labor productivity.

of agricultural and mining areas, and the demand for tools and other supplies needed for the operation of farms in conjunction with the revival and development of production.

Tracing the spread of the capitalist sprouts from the handicraft industries to the agricultural sector, Liu Yongcheng considers that the role played by the market was equally essential in agriculture. The increase in handicraft industries and the expansion of their operation required the agricultural sector to supply raw materials in ever-increasing quantities. Liu maintains that the expansion of market demand for agricultural goods stimulated the production of cash crops and the commercialization of food crops, thereby promoting improvements in agricultural technology and leading to social differentiation among the peasants. Some of the latter then emerged as managerial landlords who employed agricultural workers on money wages and grew crops mainly for the market.[2]

In the discussion of market demand, I think one more element should be added—namely, foreign trade. As I have pointed out elsewhere, foreign trade contributed to embryonic capitalism, particularly in the Jiangnan area, in two significant ways.[3] First, the unfolding of overseas trade following the Great Discoveries generated a strong demand for Chinese products such as tea, silk, and cotton goods and hence gave rise to a fair number of handicraft workshops and factories. Second, as China had always maintained a sizable favorable balance in her trade with the West and Japan before the early nineteenth century, silver in enormous amounts kept flowing into the country. The influx of the white metal helped in no small measure to ease the expanding demand for money resulting from growth of domestic trade.

Sprouts of Capitalism in Agriculture

The most striking evidence indicating capitalistic development in agriculture is the appearance of managerial landlords. In this regard, Li Wenzhi's contribution is in my judgment the most significant. He points out that as the commodity economy was expanding, the farm operation of individual peasants, which was characteristically isolated and conservative, could no longer meet the growing demand for agricultural products. Some people with entrepreneurial talents and the wherewithal were able to turn farming into a profit-making

---

[2] Liu Yongcheng, "Lun Zhongguo zibenzhuyi mengyadi lishi qianti" [On the historical prerequisite to the sprouts of capitalism in China], *Zhongguoshi yanjiu* [Studies on Chinese history], no. 2 (1979), pp. 32–46.

[3] Cf. my essay, "The Sprouts of Capitalism," in *Ming and Qing Historical Studies in the People's Republic of China*, ed. Frederic Wakeman (Berkeley: University of California Press, 1981), pp. 96–103.

business by hiring agricultural workers to produce crops for the market. Liu follows up these observations with an inquiry into the origins of the new enterprising class of managerial landlords in the countryside. Their social background can, according to him, be traced to three diverse groups: rich peasants (who originated among the poor peasants amid the commercialization of agriculture), merchants and owners of handicraft industries, and the official and gentry landlords.

What is of even greater interest are his observations on a number of social changes that affected agricultural management in the early Qing. He notes that there occurred three major developments that made it possible for capitalist sprouts to appear in agriculture, namely, changes in the distribution of landownership, changes in the composition of the landowning class, and changes in the way landownership was transferred. The government of the Ming dynasty pursued in its early decades a policy of active assistance to independent peasants; the distribution of landownership was therefore rather equitable. In the latter part of the dynasty, however, farm lands became concentrated in the hands of the privileged officials and gentry. Following a series of nationwide peasant uprisings in the early seventeenth century, which, as Liu writes, dealt a severe blow to the landlords, land distribution was once again deconcentrated. Deconcentration is asserted to lead to a weakening of feudal landlordism.

The composition of the landowning class changed at the same time, at the expense of the official and gentry landlords. That is to say, while official and gentry landlords were predominant in the Ming, commoner landlords came to the fore in the early Qing. And Li adds that most managerial landlords in Qing times were commoners. With the development of the commodity economy, farm lands became increasingly commercialized. Therefore, in contrast to the preceding periods, in which land acquisition primarily took the form of grant and commendation, landlords acquired property mainly through purchase in the Qing. According to Li, all of these developments contributed to the loosening of the feudal landholding patterns and provided conditions favorable to the growth of capitalist sprouts even in the landlord economy.

Where did incipient capitalism make its first appearance in agriculture? As I have discussed in another essay, historians in the People's Republic generally agree that the sprouts first appeared primarily in Jiangnan, though they also grew in scattered pockets outside the area. In the same essay, I also introduced Xie Guozhen's two theses—the affluence thesis and the scarcity thesis. According to Xie, the Jiangnan area was agriculturally and commercially the most developed area in China. Taking advantage of the market demand, many landlords and peasants grew cash crops and engaged in handicraft production. On the other hand, in areas such as Shanxi and Huizhou where the land was too poor to grow enough food for the consumption needs of the local population, scarcity compelled many of them to produce commodities for sale, making use of whatever raw materials (e.g., timber, bamboo) were available in the locality. Incipient capitalism could exist in both cases. In regard to the question raised above, there now appears to be a difference of opinion between two prominent economic historians. Whereas Li Wenzhi thinks that the sprouts first emerged in the most commercialized areas of Jiangsu and Zhejiang, Fu Yiling maintains, if I understand him correctly, that they first appeared in such economically backward and mountainous areas as Xincheng in Jiangxi and Nanshan Laolin, the area at the juncture of Sichuan, Shaanxi, and Hubei. That is, while Li follows the affluence thesis, Fu appears to adhere to the scarcity thesis. One can readily understand Li's position, which is probably accepted by most historians in the People's Republic. It is more difficult to comprehend Fu's statement that "China followed its own unique path of development. The laws of development were: from the mountain areas to the plains, and from cash crops to grain production. The former was unique to China, the latter was universal."[4] What Fu expounds is an elaborate version of the scarcity thesis. It is generally true that commercialization spreads from cash crops to grain production. But why did it first take place in the mountainous areas and then spread to the plains? We hope that Professor Fu will come forward with a clear explanation in the near future.

Economic Retardation

Why the capitalist sprouts failed to grow into maturity is undoubtedly the most crucial question in the whole issue of incipient capitalism. In the light of our discussions with Chinese historians and some of their recent writings on this issue, I believe that the answers given by various scholars may be reduced to three interlocking traditional institutions: landlordism, the state, and the lineage system. Li Wenzhi takes the position that under the system of landlordism, the heavy land rent exacted by landlords constituted a formidable obstacle to the rise of rich peasants. Moreover, the economy showed a strong tendency to slide backward instead of moving forward along the capitalist line because rich peasants and managerial landlords often turned themselves into renter landlords, and commoner landlords into officials and gentry landlords. Feudal landlords thus made their way back time and again rather than disappearing from the historical stage. Li therefore concludes that the problem of the long-term retardation of capitalist development in China is in the final analysis attributable to the system of the landlord economy. In his paper on the salt industry in Sichuan, Ran Guangrong also sees landlordism as detrimental to

---

[4] Fu Yiling, "Capitalism in Chinese Agriculture," *Modern China* 6, no. 3 (July 1980): 311-16.

the development of incipient capitalism: in order to control local wealth, land-lords often organized themselves into an exclusive body which prevented potential investors from developing the resources underground. Under these circumstances, it was extremely difficult for free enterprise to take root and grow.

Atop the landlord economy was a state apparatus that stood squarely behind the landlord to the disadvantage of all other social classes. A variety of views put forward by Chinese scholars support this contention. Heavy taxes imposed by the state impoverished peasants; official acquisition of commodities at prices much lower than those current in the market ruined businessmen; purchase of land and official titles by merchants in order to advance their social status inevitably reduced their capital for productive investment; and a legal code that protected employers against workers on matters relating to physical oppression and noneconomic exploitation seriously impeded the development of a free labor market.

The third institution that held the capitalist sprouts in check was lineage. The lineage system was by its very nature conservative and exerted a highly restrictive influence over human behavior. It was inimical to free enterprise, on the basis of which capitalism stands. This is why, in the opinion of Li Wenzhi, capitalism failed to develop beyond its sprouting stage in Jiangnan, even though this region was commercially the most advanced in the country. The influence of lineage was, he explains, too tenacious to be overcome in that area. More specifically, Ran Guangrong finds that the fraternal societies of salt workers in Sichuan, organized on the principle of lineage, also hindered the free movement of labor.

This brief sketch highlights the continued vigor with which Chinese historians are pursuing this historical issue. I am greatly impressed with many of the views they have put forth, most of which display great insight into the dynamism and stagnation of China's premodern economy. It is necessary to note, however, that some of their views or interpretations are of little help in understanding the problems. For example, Fu Yiling is of the opinion that the lack of industrial and commercial development in the cities caused economic retardation in the countryside. This is no doubt true, but we should first ask, and seek the answer to, why there was a lack of such development in the cities. Similarly, the hypotheses that the tenacity of feudal landlordism (Li Wenzhi) or the predominance of a self-sufficient economy (Peng Zeyi) limited the growth of capitalist sprouts throw little light on the issue. The real question is why capitalism could break through a feudalistic and self-sufficient economy in early modern Europe while it failed in China.

Moreover, some of the Chinese views may not hold since they are supported merely by anecdotal or circumstantial evidence. Were taxes so heavy that the peasants were perennially condemned to poverty? Was official acquisition of commodities at artificially low prices a common practice in the eighteenth and nineteenth centuries? Were farm lands continuously concentrated in the hands of landlords? To answer with some measure of confidence these and a number of other questions relevant to the issue of capitalist sprouts, we need well-defined (in terms of time period and geographical area) empirical and quantitative studies. And I believe that if Chinese historians direct their efforts more toward specific and quantitative research, their contributions in this area will be significantly enhanced.

SCHOLARLY AND PERSONAL COMMUNICATION
AT THE BEIJING SYMPOSIUM

William Atwell

As is evident from Professor Feuerwerker's synopsis and from the report of the Chinese side reprinted in Part III, the scholarly meetings in Beijing were conducted in a spirit of mutual respect and in an atmosphere of enormous goodwill. At one point in the proceedings an American participant was overheard to say that he had not been so nice for years, and while the same may or may not have been true of the Chinese participants (perhaps they are always that nice), the members of the American delegation were genuinely touched by the warmth and friendliness of our Chinese colleagues. Indeed, it is not exaggeration to state that participants on both sides found it difficult to say goodbye when our formal program drew to a close on the evening of 1 November.

Under these circumstances, it would, of course, be wonderful to be able to report that everything in Beijing went exactly as we had hoped and planned. However, such was not the case, and while we do not in any way wish to denigrate the efforts made on our behalf by the Chinese Academy of Social Sciences, the Committee on Scholarly Communication with the People's Republic of China, and many other organizations, we do have one or two suggestions which we hope will be taken into consideration when future conferences of this nature are being planned. First, although our gathering was quite small in comparison to other historical conferences which have been held in China recently, we still believe that there were too many people in attendance (usually about fifty) and too many papers to discuss each day (six) to allow for a completely free exchange of opinions at the formal sessions. In fact, despite the skillful and often painstaking organization of those sessions, described elsewhere in this report, authors were never able to secure sufficient time to respond formally to criticisms of their own work. Moreover, on certain occasions even those well qualified to comment on specific papers were prevented by time constraints from doing so.

For these reasons, and because it might help to alleviate some of the logistical problems which frustrated attempts to have the two delegations live and eat together in Beijing, the American side hopes that such conferences in the future can be limited to a much smaller number of formal and informal participants. If for some reason this should prove impossible, however, we then think that considerable time should be set aside for small group discussions devoted to specific papers or themes. Indeed, there are those among us who would contend that the high point of the symposium occurred on the evening of 30 October, when members of the two delegations divided into three hastily organized discussion groups to talk over problems of mutual interest, some of which had not even been raised in the formal sessions. Had there been more time to plan that evening's program, we believe that those discussions would have been even more fruitful.

These comments and suggestions should not be interpreted to mean that we consider the conference anything less than a success. To the contrary, we learned a great deal during our stay in Beijing and came away with a much better understanding of, and an enhanced appreciation for, historical scholarship in China today. In this connection, we especially appreciate the efforts made by the Chinese organizers to ensure that the younger generation of Chinese historians, about whom all too little is known outside of China, was well represented at the conference. Indeed, with due respect to the other participants, we feel that many of the best papers on the Chinese side came from this group of younger scholars. (Although the reasons for the chronological grouping are not entirely clear, those papers dealt in the main with local or regional topics in Ming and early Qing history, were very well documented—one or two awesomely so—and were generally free of the jargon which some of us have found disconcerting in certain works of Chinese scholarship in the past.) Conversations at the conference and elsewhere concerning the difficulties under which historical research is often conducted in China only served to increase our admiration for the authors' achievements.

After a somewhat hesitant first few days when the participants were getting to know one another, the conference quickly shifted into higher gear with more and more open exchanges of ideas and opinions, although the organizational difficulties and the weight of numbers mentioned above meant that time was always a problem. Particularly valuable to us, therefore, and, so far as we could ascertain, to the Chinese participants as well, were the informal conversations which were possible during the regular breaks in the formal sessions, at the banquets and other meals the two delegations had together, and at the cocktail party (jiuhui) which was hosted by CASS at the end of the conference.

Most of the Chinese scholars with whom we spoke on these occasions were very forthcoming about their current work and future research projects, and we were especially impressed by their breadth of knowledge and range of interests. For example, although most of them were, of course, primarily concerned with problems in social and economic history, several expressed the opinion that much more work needed to be done in China on premodern intellectual history in general and on political thought in particular. When it was mentioned that a number of people in the West currently were focusing their research on the so-called "statecraft" *(jingshi)* tradition in Yuan, Ming, and Qing political thought, that information was greeted with enthusiastic approval and thoughtful and incisive questions about sources, approach, and methodology.

We also found considerable support among the Chinese participants, and especially among the younger generation, for the idea that the study of certain problems in late imperial history could be enhanced by a greater awareness of historical developments in other parts of the world at approximately the same time. In this regard, we were particularly encouraged to learn that the study of foreign languages is now being required of students in certain leading history departments, that new and revised courses in world history are being introduced at a number of universities, and that new research centers dealing with foreign studies have been established or are being contemplated.

The question of comparative history also arose in connection with what is probably the most active and exciting subfield in premodern historical research in China today, that of local and regional history. One scholar told us flatly that we will never understand the Ming period until we can explain the reasons behind the very different patterns of development in the northwest and southeast of the country during the fifteenth and sixteenth centuries. (That scholar, it should be noted, is currently engaged in just such a comparative project.) Another historian applauded Professor Skinner's statement that "Jiangnan is not China" and urged Western and Chinese scholars alike to test what we have learned about that region against the materials which are available for other areas.

However, despite general agreement on these and other issues, the members of both delegations were well aware that fundamental differences between us remained on many points. Since detailed discussions of some of these differences appear elsewhere in this report, let it suffice here to mention two noteworthy examples. At the symposium, several of our Chinese colleagues complained both publicly and privately that we on the American side seemed reluctant to deal with their papers on Marxist terms. Another criticized us quite sharply for what she apparently saw as our blanket refusal to take rural poverty seriously as an issue in premodern social and economic history.

While we would not necessarily agree with these criticisms, at least not without significant qualification, some members of the American delegation were quite willing to admit that training in Marxism and Marxist historiography in the United States leaves much to be desired, a fact which undoubtedly affects our ability to respond to Marxist arguments in ways our Chinese colleagues would find more congenial. Moreover, all of us acknowledged that historians who have lived and worked in China during the past several decades are personally acquainted with poverty and hardship in ways we find difficult, if not impossible, to understand.

Having said this, however, we are not convinced that these facts impair our ability to write meaningfully about some aspects of Chinese social and economic history. Nevertheless, we are glad to have had the opportunity to explore these matters in a friendly and open manner with scholars whose historical training and personal backgrounds are so radically different from our own. There can be little doubt that we will be more sensitive to such questions in the future, which can only serve to improve our own scholarship and to enhance our understanding of the work of our Chinese friends. In this respect, as in many others, the Beijing symposium was a resounding success.

To conclude this section of our report, it perhaps would be appropriate to mention several ways in which we feel communications between Chinese and American historians can be improved. The first of these has to do with language training. As has been stressed elsewhere in this report, we were extremely fortunate in Beijing to have four native Chinese speakers among the formal and informal American participants. Without their help, and that of the patient and hard-working translators from CASS, the conference would in all probability have been a disastrous failure. Even those Americans who had spent considerable time studying in Taiwan found six days of intensive discussions in Chinese difficult to handle, particularly since few if any of them had ever attended an academic conference at which Chinese was the dominant language. Those of us who have watched our fellow Americans in Japanese studies perform in seminars and symposia in Japan are well aware of how far behind we are. The continuing opportunity to participate in conferences of this kind, will, of course, help to narrow the gap, but there is still a great deal of work to be done in our own language laboratories.

Despite the occasional problems in communication, it should be emphasized that many of the people with whom we spoke in China expressed considerable interest in the work of foreign scholars. Some of this undoubtedly was merely politeness to "foreign visitors," but we are convinced that much of it was genuine. Indeed, some members of the American delegation spent a good deal of time in Beijing answering questions not only about the current state of Chinese studies in the United States but also about work which is being done in Japan, Taiwan, Hong Kong, and Europe. Even armed with this information, however (and our Chinese colleagues took extensive notes), scholars in China confront serious obstacles in obtaining access to materials published outside the country. Not only are works in Japanese and Western languages difficult for most of them to buy or borrow, but one leading specialist in Ming history told us that he had never seen certain uncontroversial books on his subject in Chinese which are readily available in Taibei and Hong Kong bookstores. Two other scholars from major research centers said that although they knew and greatly admired the earlier work of the distinguished Hong Kong-based economic historian Quan Hansheng, they had read nothing by him which had been published since 1949.

Under these circumstances, then, it seems clear that one way we can both help our Chinese colleagues and improve scholarly communication among Chinese historians around the world is to send as much photocopied and other material to China as we and our institutions can afford. We were told before leaving Beijing that provided such materials were historical in nature and not concerned with contemporary affairs, they would reach their destinations without much difficulty. (Subsequent experience has borne this out, although Western-language materials apparently pass through the Chinese postal service much more slowly than those in Chinese or Japanese.) For those wondering where to begin, we were informed that bibliographies and book lists of all sorts would be especially welcome.

Finally, we would like to note that while we are naturally pleased that Professor Wang Yuquan and other members of the Chinese delegation found our research methods "worthy of . . . consideration and adoption," we are fully aware that we still have a great deal more to learn from them than they do from us. Our experiences at the discussion sessions in Beijing, and especially our contacts with the extremely talented younger historians there, convince us that, barring unforeseen catastrophes, they will be willing and stimulating teachers for many years to come.

HISTORY FROM TWO DIMENSIONS:
A HISTORIAN'S VIEW OF THE SYMPOSIUM

Evelyn S. Rawski

In his concluding speech at the symposium, the distinguished economic historian Yan Zhongping, chairman of the Chinese delegation, pointed to a major difference between American sinological studies and the work of Chinese scholars. Yan began by praising the breadth and diversity of the topics treated and analytical methods used in the American papers, but, he observed, we cannot and should not assume that historical reality lies in the sum total of monographic research on demography, price history, monetary history, and the like. We must ask, what is the ultimate significance of this search for historical understanding? Unless historical phenomena are organized around a central unifying theme or axis, we cannot obtain an integrated picture of past societies.

For historians working in the People's Republic of China, this unifying axis for historical work has been and continues to be the issue of class and class struggle. Yan continued by saying that American historians need not adopt the same focus but should nonetheless recognize the necessity for a central organizing principle in historical analysis. How else can phenomena over time be studied?

International conferences can provide insight into a discipline's preoccupations and orientations that are readily apparent to outsiders, if not to those living within the culture. Yan's comment about the lack of a unified history in the United States is, of course, quite correct. Here, as in Europe, the growth of social science orientations has been accompanied by an atomization of historical studies. Monographic research blossoms, but Western historical writing tends more and more to be content with microcosmic analysis that bypasses the larger synthesis that surely should lie at the core of our research efforts. Indeed, most historians no longer feel that they need to justify their specialized research by linking it to a larger framework, and it is difficult to see how American historians could be brought to agree on a common unifying theme for their work.

Of course, the atomization of history is not unique; we see the same trend in many fields. We are told that in some natural sciences specialization has proceeded to the point where members of the same field with different specialties can no longer understand each other's work. The consequence of such specialization is the narrowing of readership. Carlyle was read by all educated Englishmen; today, my colleagues complain that the best historical research (judged by the standards of the profession) is read only by a small group of historians, while popular history tends to be inferior in quality. That this need not always be the case is illustrated by the French regard for history and the high praise they have conferred upon Emmanuel Le Roy Ladurie, but in the United States we do not have Laduries who enjoy the same status. Our own relative isolation in American culture suggests that we should seriously consider Yan's observation and think about the ultimate meaning of our scholarship.

For their part, Americans emerged from the symposium with observations concerning the preoccupations of their Chinese counterparts. Why, for example, has so little work been done recently in China on what we in the West see as major topics—historical demography, price history, monetary history, analysis of marketing hierarchies and macroregional systems, or the anthropologically oriented social history currently in vogue? We know that it is not paucity of data that holds back research, because many materials exist within China that could support study of these topics.

But for Chinese historians such topics have only peripheral relevance for the central issue that has dominated Chinese historical analysis since 1949: class struggle as the dynamic force in history. Chinese historians reiterated their commitment to this focus throughout the conference, both in their own papers and in their comments on American contributions. Why, they asked, did Americans place so much emphasis on marketing as a basic principle of spatial and social organization? From their point of view, this emphasis is misplaced because it focuses on the circulation of commodities as opposed to the production of goods. As Feuerwerker noted at one session, the Chinese treatment of commerce is ambiguous. In general, Chinese scholars ignore the role of distribution of goods in the economy; some do study ouput, but most do not even do that, concentrating instead on the class relations in the process of production. The different orientations of Chinese and American scholars were clearly revealed in the discussions of marketing.

Chinese emphasis on class struggle has resulted in a concentration of research on certain subjects, for example, peasant uprisings, the tyranny of the feudal state, and the exploitation and oppression of peasants by feudal landlords. Here again, Americans and Chinese expressed sharply different views of the significance of published work on each topic. Where several Americans suggested that the Chinese state, especially in late imperial times, was weak rather than strong when compared to Japan or states in Europe, Chinese historians reiterated their conviction that the state was extremely strong. Where American scholars stressed the relative improvement of tenancy conditions in late Ming and early Qing times, most Chinese historians stressed the existence into the twentieth century of semiservile dependent households, such as the *dianpu* of Huizhou in Anhui province.

Chinese orientations also shaped selection of data within the topics studied. In peasant uprisings, for example, Chinese scholars generally reject the notion that such uprisings could be led by members of the elite. They reject the notion that religion could motivate believers to rebel. From their perspective, religion is a tool used by the elite to manipulate and control the masses and cannot explain genuinely dissident behavior on the part of commoners. Similarly, the search for exploitation in tenancy systems has led to extensive landlord account books and rent rolls which might offer a basis for investigating enforcement of the contract as opposed to the legal stipulations of the contract itself. Detailed analysis of the frequency of rent arrears and general study of the complete landlord economy have not been prominent elements in Chinese research on traditional agriculture.

The contrast between Chinese research, based on a unified view of history, and the American hypothesis-testing, social science approach was made very clear in discussions on interpretation of data. These differences were sharpened by the very different training to be found in China and the United States. American historians interested in social science research are sensitive to the need for disciplinary training in a social science, whether it be economics, sociology, anthropology, or anything else. Most would agree that acquaintance with statistical methods is highly desirable, if not mandatory. Chinese historians, by contrast, have had virtually no social science training; this is inevitable given the political disturbances of the 1960s and the rejection of "bourgeois" methodology in the social sciences.

The differences in training, coupled with different perspectives, have led to different evaluations of data. In general, Chinese historians were critical of the large-scale quantitative analyses presented by several American participants. Use of statistical tests to accept or reject data did not seem to be part of their historical apparatus, nor was there any awareness of the use of sampling techniques. The result was that Chinese comments tended to ignore or reject certain primary sources: for example, one discussant of Yeh-chien Wang's paper on Qing grain prices cited known instances of inconsistency in the grain price reports as proof that the abundant price citations found in archival records could not be reliably used. Americans, for their part, were critical of Chinese attempts to draw conclusions concerning the whole Ming-Qing agricultural economy from case studies of Huizhou dependent households. Here the American stress on the need to answer the question of how representative a given historical case is of the whole (largely unverifiable) historical reality ran at cross purposes with the Chinese vision of class conflict as the dominant motivating force in history. In the latter instance, significance becomes verification of the historical vision, representativeness a question of the degree to which a given piece of historical reality confirms or disputes this vision. Americans and Chinese thus have very different tests for historical significance. An oversimplified generalization would be that to the Chinese scholar, American historians pursue trivial questions with an absurdly elaborate statistical apparatus, while to Americans, Chinese historians do not conduct real research because their conclusions precede their data collection and analysis.

Is there any alternative to the Chinese focus on class struggle for Chinese historians? As K. C. Liu has noted, recent policy shifts away from class struggle to emphasis on the forces of production have been reflected in historical articles pointing to the desirability of studying the forces of production in history and production struggle, but it is difficult to envisage an abandonment of class struggle as the ultimate historical theme in the near future.

Chinese historians are still caught up (for obvious reasons) in asking why China, an advanced civilization, did not develop the momentum that would have nurtured its capitalist sprouts into long-term transformation of the traditional agricultural and handicraft economy. Why didn't China have an industrial revolution? The relative neglect of comparative analysis in the work on this question requires further explanation. Why have Chinese historians rejected the notion that "feudal" China can and should be compared with "feudal" Europe? Why have they so frequently clung to the argument that China is a special case? Why, given their own framework, have Chinese historians displayed so little interest in the work of European Marxist historians? Why, to go further, do they reveal only slight acquaintance with Marx's own writings about the emergence of capitalism and his unrivaled descriptions of the dynamic power of this new phenomenon to transform traditional society and economy? The notion that China is a "special case" seems to outside observers a hindrance to further scholarly advance.

The Sino-American Symposium on Chinese Social and Economic History from the Song to 1900 represented a real advance in communication between Chinese and American historians. It helped each side to understand better the cultural constraints under which we all work by exposure to the widely different orientations of the historians from each country. These differences were obvious, but it would be a mistake to assume monolithic unity in the scholarship of either country. Chinese historians talked about their own scholarly disputes and debates, just as Americans expressed differing views among themselves. The future holds hope that as such scholarly exchanges continue and expand, so will the dimensions of our historical understanding of the Chinese past.

PART II:
ABSTRACTS OF THE SYMPOSIUM PAPERS

The abstracts of the papers by the American participants were prepared by the individual authors. The abstracts of the Chinese papers are either translations of abstracts provided by the authors or summaries of the original papers prepared under the direction of Professor G. William Skinner, who organized the collection and editing of the materials in Part II. The abstracts are arranged alphabetically by author's surname.

TIME AND MONEY:
ANOTHER APPROACH TO THE PERIODIZATION OF MING HISTORY

William S. Atwell

Originally inspired by Willard J. Peterson's provocative "Ming Periodization: An Immodest Proposal" (*Ming Studies*, Fall 1976), this paper begins by dividing Ming history into eight periods based on statistical information relating to domestic mining, bullion imports, and the amounts of silver circulating within the Ming monetary system. This is followed by a chronological discussion of each of these eight periods which attempts to determine whether the periodization scheme makes sense when other factors are taken into consideration.

While acknowledging both the inadequacy of the statistics currently available on the Ming economy and the validity of Christopher Hill's warning that the "connection between economies and politics is not simple," the paper tentatively concludes that silver and its role in the Ming monetary system should not be overlooked in any effort to arrive at a general understanding of the dynamics of the dynasty's economic, social, and even political history. Indeed, many of the things for which the Ming is best known—the Cheng Ho expeditions, the construction of Peking, the manufacture of exquisite porcelain, the boom in the textile industry, rapid population growth, and the implementation of the single-whip method of taxation—all appear to have occurred mainly during periods in which domestic mining, bullion imports, or a combination of the two were providing substantial amounts of silver for governmental and private use.

There can be little doubt that too much bullion in circulation and sharp fluctuations in the money supply's rate of growth eventually did the Ming economy considerable harm. Still, it is hard to imagine what that economy would have been like had the restrictive mining and commercial policies of early Ming leaders prevailed. That the latter of those policies did not prevail owed more than a little to developments in other parts of the world over which the Ming government had virtually no control. Indeed, the eagerness of foreign merchants to exchange their silver for Chinese goods during this period helped to involve China more deeply in world economic affairs than ever before, a fact of critical importance not only for periodizing Ming history but also for understanding the significant role played by the Ming empire in world history during the momentous transition from "Middle Ages" to "modern times."

THE SYSTEM OF TAX ON GRAIN TRANSPORTED FROM SOUTH CHINA VIA THE GRAND CANAL DURING THE MING DYNASTY

Bao Yanbang

This essay investigates the Ming system of grain tribute (*caoliang*) and the ruinous effects of the burden it imposed upon the peasantry. Four major issues are discussed: the nature and purpose of the grain tribute, its assessment and collection, its shipment and the costs of transportation, and other related but extraneous burdens. My views on these issues are summarized below.

First, grain tribute during the Ming was that portion of the land tax designated for delivery to the capital from the six provinces of South Zhili, Zhejiang, Jiangxi, Huguang, Henan, and Shandong. It was a substantial burden for the taxpayers, especially those in the first two provinces. For one thing, unlike the land tax in general, the grain tribute could be neither remitted nor reduced even in times of natural calamities since it was allocated to the critical consumption needs of officials in the capital and troops on the northern frontier. Moreover, since most of the grain tribute came from South Zhili and Zhejiang, the taxpayers in these areas had to bear disproportionately high tax rates. They were also required to pay for the costs of transportation from the point of collection to the capital—costs that were several times the value of the grain tribute itself.

Second, above and beyond its food supply function, the grain tribute system was designed to raise additional government revenues. Under the system, 4 million *shi* of tribute grain and more than 20,000 *shi* of fine polished rice (known as *bailiang*) were collected from the six targeted provinces. Transport costs were borne by the peasants of these provinces in the form of a surcharge for wastage. Furthermore, the government continually levied surcharges and, through such devices as "converting surcharges into taxes per se," used them to pay for official salaries, frontier defense, boat repairs, etc. In this way, the grain tribute system became a fiscal instrument used to alleviate the ever-growing deficit of the Ming government. The system was plagued by extortion of all kinds on the part of the local officials, officers, and soldiers in charge of grain transportation and the yamen clerks and runners assigned to assess and collect the grain tribute.

Finally, although large landowners were by regulation liable for the payment of grain tribute, they generally managed, in collusion with officials, to evade the tax. This resulted in an even greater burden on the peasantry. Statistics in the Ming historical record indicate that the real burden on the taxpayer was three to six times the grain tribute proper. Such an onerous and exploitative tax could not but have a significant impact on the conditions of the economy and on class struggle.

In the overpopulated prefectures of Suzhou and Songjiang, the heavy burden of taxation forced the peasants to engage in handicraft production (particularly spinning and weaving) in order to earn the extra income needed to maintain a minimum level of subsistence. In effect, therefore, the exploitation of peasants by the Ming government extended beyond agriculture to subsidiary handicraft industries as well. In exchanging the cloth they produced for money, the peasants were subject to the vicissitudes of the commodity market and the exploitation of usurious merchants. Many of them were financially ruined and abandoned their land, especially after the middle of the Ming. There were numerous instances in which peasants bitterly resisted the collection of taxes and rent in grain tribute provinces. This resistance movement was a direct threat to the Ming rulers.

A PRELIMINARY ANALYSIS OF
TENANT-LANDLORD RELATIONSHIPS IN MING AND QING CHINA

Fu-mei Chang Chen

Chinese historians writing about tenant-landlord relations in the 1950s and 1960s emphasized the exploitative aspects, whereas those writing more recently, especially in the context of analyzing incipient capitalist development, have tended to downplay exploitation. This paper confronts this contradiction by examining surviving Qing contracts in order to clarify the terms of property rights between landlords and tenants. The findings suggest that earlier scholarship may have exaggerated the degree of exploitation.

This essay treats topics such as multiple landownership, share rent versus fixed crop rent, flexibility in rent payment, vulnerability of landlords in dealing with tenants, and so forth. Although many of the examples come from Taiwan, which is hardly a representative Chinese province, the contractual relations revealed by the Taiwanese contracts all have counterparts elsewhere in China.

The existence of permanent tenancy and multiple landownership rights in many areas of China attests to the fact that several households often did lay claim to a single plot of land and derive a stream of income from it. Because land, a scarce resource, provided income and appreciated in value over time, the Chinese developed a unique arrangement of sharing rights to land so that an expanded number of households could benefit from the income it produced. With multiple property rights, a delicate balance had to be maintained among all parties to the contract. It is clear from the terms of these contracts that the various parties were keenly aware of the interdependence that derived from their property rights. They displayed a fine sense of equity and fair play, and they accepted frequent adjustments to the terms of contract in order to keep the agreements mutually beneficial to all parties. These corrective measures varied considerably; some appear to have been prompted by the deliberate intent of one party, others not.

KAIFENG AROUND THE ELEVENTH CENTURY

Chen Zhen

Since Northern Song Kaifeng was the first city in the world to free itself from an early medieval urban form, it has been the subject of many studies by both Chinese and foreign scholars. It goes without saying that the scope, form, appearance, and structure of a city reflect the level of development of the forces and relations of production.

Population. We find two opposing tendencies in treating the population of Song cities. One ignores official population statistics altogether and relies instead on contemporary or later estimates. The other relies solely on official statistics, disregarding unrealistic features of the data. Katō Shigeshi concludes that, while official Song statistics may be reasonably accurate in enumerating households, they undercount the number of persons. He believes household size averaged well over five persons, rising to twenty or more in the case of officials' households. This accords with reality and should be used in evaluating Song urban population statistics. Katō argues that as cities grew, the number of officials and rich families also grew, and he therefore estimates household size at six members in a city of average size, seven in a large city. In 1021, official statistics gave a figure of 97,750 households in Kaifeng proper. If suburban districts, soldiers and their dependents, monks, and transients are added in, there must have been at least 1.2 million people inhabiting the city.

Handicraft Workplaces. Kaifeng had many official factories employing more than a thousand men each. In 1048, the Dusheng and five other privately owned workplaces in Kaifeng remitted taxes and goods valued at 158,340 strings of cash (equivalent to 18,991 English ounces of gold). Obviously, their scope was very large. Handicraft workplaces usually contained several workshops, with a finely drawn division of labor among workers. The Eastern Brick Factory had ten categories of workers, including tile makers, brick makers, and decorated tile makers, which approximates the division of labor in modern brick and tile factories. The most important sector of the labor force in official factories was construction workers, who were garrison troops, but official factories also used hired labor. For example, in 1007 the Duquyuan was said to have "hired civilian workers." Hiring laborers from among the people must have been widespread. Competition was very fierce, which is the principal reason why Dusheng and other civilian factories almost squeezed out the official factories. These comparatively free workers and their wage structure display some obviously modern characteristics despite the persistence of strong feudal relationships of production.

The Urban System. It is clear from the demise of the ward system that Kaifeng was moving away from early medieval urban structures. The first manifestations of a new urban system were the police patrols and fire brigades established in the late tenth century as part of the cavalry's public security system. In 995 the garrison troops were reorganized into several levels, and in 1070 separate district-level commands were established for garrisons of the left and the right. These were part of the administrative system of Kaifeng prefecture. Early in the eleventh century, garrisons in both the city proper and in the suburbs were controlled by Kaifeng prefecture. In the Xining period (1068-1077), this structure was altered so that, while forces in the city proper remained under the prefecture, those in the extramural suburbs and in the countryside were placed under the control of surrounding counties. A household registration system for urban residents only was established early in the eleventh century.

In summary, eleventh-century Kaifeng already manifested protocapitalist elements in its relationships of production, and its urban system had evolved distinctly modern characteristics.

TWO EXAMPLES OF THE DEVELOPMENT OF CITIES IN THE SONG DYNASTY

Cheng Yingliu

The development of Song cities has attracted the interest of many Chinese and foreign scholars. This paper deals with two topics within this general subject that have not been adequately studied previously: service agents *(jiandang guan)* and borough officials *(xiangguan)*.

The post of service agent, whose function was to control the monopoly tax bureaus in Song cities, was filled by ranked officials serving the court or stationed at the capital *(jingchao guan)* or by palace intendants of the inner palace *(neishi shi)*. This use of eunuchs, with their close palace connections, and of high officials indicates the importance attached to this post by the government. The Northern Song stress on this office was one aspect of the general Song policy of recentralization.

An understanding of this office is important in studying the development of Song cities because of its connection with commercial taxes. While commercial taxes were hardly new, they took on unprecedented fiscal importance during the Song. As the early Song established control over commerce, a host of miscellaneous taxes were abolished, and the tax on trade was greatly increased. The prefectures and subprefectures all had officials to oversee the trade-tax bureaus. More important prefectures sometimes had two officials, one civil and one military, whereas in smaller subprefectures the duties of the service agent might be given concurrently to an official holding another position.

Revenues were generated in these cities by the presence of markets, which were sometimes open both day and night and often specialized in certain products, such as meat or fresh fish. Cities also taxed commerce through such institutions as the guilds *(hang)*, associations *(tuan)* for trade, and entertainment centers *(wa)*. The accelerating pace of commerce was reflected in the growing numbers of periodic markets and fairs.

Another topic worthy of further attention is the role of borough officials in cities. The Northern Song capital, Kaifeng, had four intramural boroughs. In 1008 eight boroughs were ordered established outside the city wall, where previously there had been only a sheriff to oversee the growing population. A document from 1021 indicates that suburban boroughs incorporated from 4,000 to nearly 9,000 households. They were subdivided into wards (fang), ranging in number from seven to twenty-six. Each borough had a differentiated staff of twenty to more than thirty functionaries. The four boroughs within the capital walls were overseen by the assistant prefect (tongpan) of the capital prefecture and his subordinate subprefects.

The Southern Song capital, Lin'an (Hangzhou), had nine boroughs. Each had a lesser military envoy (xiao shichen) who oversaw officials in charge of fire and police protection. There is some indication that certain kinds of lawsuits could be handled at this level. Borough affairs were also at least partly under the jurisdiction of borough surveillance officers (xiang yuhou) and patrolling inspectors (xunjian), chosen from among military officers. Each borough contained a number of police posts (pu).

This division of cities into boroughs was not restricted to the imperial capitals. We know, for instance, that both Shaoxing and Ningbo were divided into boroughs and wards.

A PRELIMINARY STUDY OF THE DEVELOPMENT OF THE COTTON PLANTING AND TEXTILE INDUSTRIES DURING THE MING DYNASTY

Cong Hanxiang

Cotton cultivation spread during the Song and Yuan periods, and by Ming times cotton was grown throughout China. An examination of more than 250 local gazetteers from this period indicates that one quarter to one third of all counties in the empire produced cotton.

The provinces, prefectures, and counties for which evidence of cotton cultivation is available and the source of the evidence for each area are identified in table 1 (not included here). With the possible exception of Guizhou, for which the evidence is unclear, all provinces contained cotton-producing areas. However, the distribution and area of production was very unequal. This variation may be usefully characterized in terms of three separate blocks of provinces.

The North China region consists of the five provinces of Shandong, Henan, North Zhili, Shanxi, and Shaanxi. Of these, Shandong and Henan were the largest cotton producers—first in the country—and North Zhili was next in line. The adjacent areas of northwestern Shandong, northeastern Henan, and the southern part of North Zhili comprised the richest cotton region in all of China. This portion of the North China Plain has ideal conditions for cotton cultivation.

The Middle and Lower Yangzi region consists of the provinces of South Zhili, Zhejiang, Huguang, and Jiangxi. Songjiang prefecture was at the center of the Jiangnan production area. Cotton cultivation had a long history there, and in the Ming period this was one of the major growing areas in China.

The South and Southwest China region is comprised of Fujian, Guangdong, Guangxi, Yunnan, and Sichuan. Not much is known about cotton cultivation in Guangxi, Yunnan, and Sichuan. In Guangdong, cotton was widely planted, but the total production was not substantial. Cotton cultivation in Fujian was confined mainly to the east and north of the province.

Cotton textile manufacturing spread across China in conjunction with the expansion of cotton cultivation. This was the most important handicraft industry during the Ming period. Table 2 (not included here) identifies the provinces, prefectures, and counties for which evidence of cotton cloth production is available and cites the source of the evidence for each area. It was rare for the textile industry to develop beyond a negligible level in areas where cotton was not produced. Areas with a modest output of cotton generally supported a limited textile industry. Interestingly, areas boasting both a rich output of cotton and fully developed textile manufacturing were few. An examination of conditions in each province shows how cotton textiles were produced.

In the Ming period, production of cotton cloth remained a sideline cottage industry. Although there were some specialized manufacturers, they had neither shops nor hired laborers. A cottage textile industry also appeared early in the history of other countries, but the system found in China has some distinctive features. First, in all areas where enabling conditions obtained, north or south, rich or poor, almost all rural households produced cotton cloth. Even in Jiangnan, the most developed production area, it remained a cottage industry. Second, this mode of production enabled the feudal government to further its exploitation of poor peasants. Women and children contributed their labor by spinning and weaving for many hours each day. Their earnings, however meager, became an important source of household income for peasants with very little land, helping them endure the hardships of feudal exploitation. Finally, when pursued by peasant households, cotton textile manufacturing involved minimal additional costs. In consequence, other forms of handicraft production, particularly factories employing wage labor, could hardly compete. This is one important reason for the underdevelopment of industry in old China.

THE RELATIONSHIP OF THE MERCENARY SYSTEM OF THE NORTHERN SONG PERIOD TO SOCIAL WEAKNESSES, POVERTY, AND AGRICULTURAL PRODUCTION

Deng Guangming

This essay deals with an important and hitherto little-studied aspect of Northern Song history, the military recruitment system and its impact on the government and economy of that era.

The study falls into two major parts. The first discusses the military recruitment system and its political consequences. While ostensibly designed to achieve the usual goals of a military system—the defense of the state against external or internal unrest, the Song system was also utilized to achieve a number of important hidden objectives. In particular, the recruitment system may be shown to have been used by Song rulers to: (1) create a set of checks and balances between high-level civil bureaucrats and the generals of the palace armies; (2) create a stable balance between the garrisons at the capital and those stationed in the provinces; (3) prevent collusion between generals and their men; (4) prevent an alliance between the generals and the head of the Bureau of Military Affairs; and (5) divide the peasantry against itself by drawing a large group of peasants into full-time, long-term military service, which led them to support the state even against their fellow peasants.

The second part treats the unintended economic and fiscal consequences of the system. Although it was strikingly successful in achieving its intended political goals, the system also generated some undesirable consequences. For whatever reason, the state opted for quantity rather than quality: it created larger and larger armies but failed to develop an adequate training program. As a result, the great size of the armies turned out to be a source of weakness. Although at its largest the Song military establishment included more than 1.3 million soldiers, it still proved inadequate.

The weakness of the Song military was accompanied by great fiscal weakness. This fiscal weakness, and the relationship of defense costs to it, has been discussed by many commentators from Song times onward. Materials adduced here confirm the traditional analysis.

Finally, the essay raises the possibility that the Song military recruitment system hindered agricultural productivity and development by withdrawing large numbers of able-bodied men from the labor force, thereby creating an agricultural labor shortage. The evidence presented suggests that this problem was especially acute in the heartland of the empire, where there appears to have been so serious a shortage that some fertile land was abandoned and returned to wasteland.

SOCIAL STRUCTURE, KINSHIP, AND LOCAL-LEVEL POLITICS
IN MING AND QING CHINA

Jerry Dennerline

This paper argues for the need to "rethink" local history in China and is divided into three parts. Part 1 is a discussion of revisionist developments within social anthropology with respect to political systems, kinship, normativeness, and social networks. This rethinking has stimulated development of such concepts as political field, in which historical association and organizational strategies, rather than normative categories, determine rules; and personal networks or quasi-groups, in which personal relationships as well as structural or categorical relationships determine political action. It is argued that these concepts are especially well suited to the study of local history in China.

Part 2 introduces several anthropological and historical studies of Chinese communities and kinship groups, showing how interaction between the fields of history and anthropology is becoming increasingly necessary for research in either field. Historical questions are raised in the work of such anthropologists as Freedman, Cohen and Pasternak, and anthropological issues are raised in the work of such historians as Beattie, Johanna Meskill, and myself. It is argued that the patterns described in the work of these scholars are sufficiently varied to make current generalizations about the history of "gentry society" premature.

Part 3 discusses patterns of centrality within one higher-order lineage (the Hua) and related patterns of centrality within the community of which that lineage was a part (Dangkou, Wuxi county), relations between the community and outsiders, and types of local leadership from the Yuan period to 1900. It is argued that significant structural changes occurred in both the lineage and the community at several points over the five-hundred-year period, that each entailed the legitimation of power held by an emergent group within the lineage or the community or both, and that this power in each case derived from successful organizational strategies that can be understood only in the local historical context.

THE RISE AND DEVELOPMENT OF THE "SINGLE-WHIP" TAX REFORM (YITIAOBIAN FA)

Fan Shuzhi

At the beginning of the Ming dynasty (1368-1644), the service levies (yi) required of able-bodied males in the population were irregularly imposed, and the frequency of actual service was low. As time went by, however, the variety and frequency of services demanded by the bureaucracy increased, and inequalities in the service levy system became even more pronounced. In order to counter this trend, the so-called junyao (equal service) reforms were implemented during the Zhengtong reign (1436-1449). New service lists were compiled and the basis for service levies was changed to take into account both landholding and the available number of able-bodied males.

During the Hongzhi (1488-1505) and Zhengde (1506-1521) eras, the commutation of service levy obligations to payments in silver began, a development which was in keeping with the increased monetarization of the economy and the tendency to commute more and more taxes into silver payments. This trend reached a logical conclusion with the implementation of the so-called "single-whip method" (yitiaobian fa) of taxation during the Jiajing (1522-1566) and Wanli (1573-1620) reigns. Prior to its empirewide promulgation during the Wanli period, the single-whip method had been used for many years in Zhejiang province in order to consolidate the service levies and provide for more uniform tax payments in silver.

As this paper demonstrates, one of the more important features of the single-whip method was that it corrected some of the more noticeable inequalities in the service levy burden, changing the basis of those levies even more firmly than before to both land and the availability of able-bodied males. And despite its many inadequacies, the single-whip method's commutation of various types of service levies into silver payments, its consolidation of such payments with those for taxes on land, and its attempts to impose some uniformity on a very complex system of taxation make it an extremely important development in Chinese history.

Nevertheless, this paper goes on to show that while it dealt effectively with the irregular service levies, the single-whip method had no effect on most regular service levies. Reform of these levies was the object of the *juntian junyi* (equalization) system which was implemented in some parts of the country during the late Ming and early Qing periods. This system was in fact an extension of the single-whip method, with service obligations once again based on land and able-bodied males. The next logical step would have been to base taxes solely upon land, which, as is discussed at the conclusion of the paper, the *tanding rudi* and *diding heyi* reforms of the Qing period sought to achieve. Indeed, it can be said that from the Tang period (618-906) on, the overall trend in China was in the direction of consolidated taxes. The single-whip method, an important milestone in this development, demonstrates very clearly the close relationship which existed between taxes and land.

THE STATE AND THE ECONOMY IN LATE IMPERIAL CHINA

Albert Feuerwerker

A number of ways in which the Chinese state in the Song, Ming, and Qing dynasties interacted with the economy are considered in the context of the potential means by which any premodern state may influence a premodern economy. The Chinese historical experience is compared with that of early modern Europe from the fifteenth to the eighteenth century.

The limited direct influence of the state on the Chinese economy before recent times is suggested by estimating the proportion of government revenue (taxes and labor services) to national income in the Song, Ming, and Qing periods. Hazardous guesses, to be sure, but sound enough to give some support to the conclusion that in premodern China, as in premodern Europe, there was a "natural limit" (perhaps 5 to 7 percent) on the proportion of the national product that the government could extract directly from the economy. Some speculations are offered to relate this limit to constraints on the state's span of control in premodern societies, which itself may be associated with economic and demographic limits on the premodern rate of urbanization.

Varieties of indirect influence on the economy are considered next, i.e., measures or policies other than the collection and disbursement of tax revenues. China's economy from the Song onward was essentially a market economy, it is argued, in which most of the economic results were determined by decisions made and actions taken in the private sector. These government policies—which varied in object and intensity over the centuries, reflecting the structure of politics and the interplay of social forces—do not seem to have hindered China's premodern economic growth (i.e., increases in population and total output but not in output per capita) and may at times have facilitated it. Finally, the influence of the government, direct and indirect, on agriculture and on commerce is considered in somewhat greater detail, again with comparisons made to contemporary European experience.

The principal conclusions of the paper can be summed up as follows. (1) China's premodern economic growth from the Song onward was remarkable though uneven in both rate and locale. (2) The policies and actions of the imperial government, insofar as they concern premodern economic growth, were not unusual when compared to the early modern European experience. On balance, they probably helped rather than hindered the long-term increase of population and total output. (3) Neither the direct nor indirect influences of the state on the economy were the major factors determining the nature and rate of growth. This was decided largely by the dynamics of the dominant private sector of the economy. (4) Toward modern economic growth ("development," i.e., increases in per capita output), the state contributed little if anything, in contrast to the history of early modern Europe. But its failings were probably less those of exploitation and corruption—the "feudal autocracy" emphasized by many Chinese historians—than those of omission and incompetence.

WASTELAND RECLAMATION POLICIES AND ACHIEVEMENTS DURING THE REIGNS OF SHUNZHI (1644-1661) AND KANGXI (1662-1722)

Guo Songyi

In China, the rise and fall of a feudal dynasty were often directly related to the level of agricultural production. Thus, in order to consolidate their control and ensure a solid basis for future exploitation, the rulers of a new dynasty gave high priority to the restoration of agriculture and the development of production. During the late Ming and early Qing, production was badly damaged and land abandoned. But by the end of the Kangxi reign, the feudal economy had fully recovered and, indeed, achieved new heights. Qing policies on land reclamation thus had major significance. What were these policies? What were their consequences?

The Qing had to cope with the economic devastation resulting from civil war, mirrored in very large tax arrears. They also had to solve the problem of homeless peasants, a potential threat to public order. Basic reclamation policies were adopted in the Shunzhi reign, namely, the right to settle on unowned, untilled lands, liberal time extensions on tax remissions, and official loans for the purchase of cattle, seed, and tools. In this period, however, it was difficult to implement these policies because of the military campaigns that were being waged as part of the Qing conquest. The state could not afford to fulfill its promises on tax remissions and therefore ignored them. The same problem obstructed loans for seed, oxen, and tools. Government attempts to establish military colonies (tuntian) as a means of settling land and solving the problem of military provisioning also failed, because the burden put on the colonists was very heavy and many ran away when taxes were due. This program was abandoned, and many of the tuntian were converted to private land. State policy shifted to encouraging landlords and gentry to invite peasants to settle abandoned lands. Unable to provide the capital itself, the state planned to have the private sector carry out the task of reclamation.

There are two basic reasons for the failure of the Shunzhi policies for land reclamation: the first is the instability of the social environment, and the second is the many alterations in policy. The dynasty was not yet in a position to provide the stability required for economic normalcy, and the fluctuations in policy were linked to the course of continuing civil strife.

PATTERNS OF SETTLEMENT, THE STRUCTURE OF GOVERNMENT, AND THE SOCIAL TRANSFORMATION OF THE CHINESE ELITE, CA. 750-1550

Robert M. Hartwell

During the period from 750 to 1550, significant regional variations in the patterns of Chinese settlement depended upon (1) the selective impact on agriculture of man-made or natural catastrophes (e.g., the rebellion of Huang Chao at the end of the Tang, the Mongol wars of the thirteenth century, and the floods associated with the 1194 shift in the course of the Yellow River) and (2) the differential effects of the introduction of novel agricultural technology (e.g., new varieties of rice seed in the late Tang, Ten Kingdoms, and early Song periods). Within regions, the hierarchy of central places was associated with the gradient of agricultural productivity, and prevailing migration was from areas of high fertility to contiguous marginal lands. There were, of course, special cases, such as the rise of exceptionally large cities which resulted from the designation of a site as an imperial capital or from the development of a port as a center of international commerce.

Catastrophes led to sequences of larger or shorter cycles of development—temporary migration to "safe" areas, abandonment of marginal lands, return after normal conditions were reestablished, and resettlement of marginal lands. But these cycles also played a role in the permanent expansion of the densely settled areas of the empire—migrants reclaimed land, invested in improvements such as roads, dikes, and irrigation networks, and created the political security needed for productive economic activity. After favorable conditions had been restored in the formerly troubled region, a portion of the migrant population remained in the newly colonized area and in due course spread from the most fertile lands to the marginal periphery. The settlement of coastal Lingnan during the Song-Yuan-Ming transition is a good example of this process. The introduction of new agricultural technology accelerated the process of migration of surplus population from areas of traditional settlement to those where the novel methods were most effective and extended the limits of the natural increase of population in this frontier zone. During the period under investigation in this paper, the combined effects of catastrophe and innovation in agricultural technique resulted in dramatic population growth

93

within four southerly macroregions—the Middle Yangzi, the Lower Yangzi, the Southeast Coast, and Lingnan.

The altered economic and demographic map of China created serious strains within the governmental structure that had been created in Qin-Han times. During the eleventh, twelfth, and thirteenth centuries, there was a progressive erosion of the ability of the central organs of imperial administration to manage the daily affairs of the disparate regions of the empire. By the early Ming, the *xian* had replaced the *zhou* (or *jun*) as the most important unit of local government, and the province *(sheng)* had replaced the center as the primary focus of administration for most large regions of China.

The new demographic, economic, and governmental conditions that emerged during the Tang, Song, Yuan, and early Ming periods resulted in a transformation in the composition and behavior of the political elite. During all periods of Chinese history, there had been a close correlation between the population density of an area and the size and influence of its local elite or gentry. The colonization of new regions and the general growth of population during the period from 750 to 1550 was accompanied by a dramatic expansion in the geographical distribution and absolute number of families that achieved elite status. At the same time, there was a major shift in the strategies of those families that had hitherto monopolized the highest positions in the imperial administration. Up to the end of the eleventh century, a so-called "aristocracy" comprised of great families from disparate regions of the empire specialized in government service, intermarried with one another so as to perpetuate their political power, and maintained and expanded their economic position through the rewards and prerogatives provided by appointment to high office. During the eleventh and twelfth centuries, the decline in the real importance of the central government, combined with the insecurity created by recurring factional power struggles and their accompanying purges, caused these families to abandon their traditional patterns of contracting interregional marriage alliances so as to gain empirewide political advantage in favor of marriage connections with elite families from their native districts in order to perpetuate their *local* political influence and economic position. At the same time, they adopted the lineage strategy favored by the local gentry whereby political careers were designated for only a portion of their male progeny.

THE DEVELOPMENT OF INDUSTRY AND COMMERCE AND THE SPROUTS OF CAPITALISM IN SUZHOU DURING THE MING AND QING DYNASTIES

Hong Huanchun

The most important primary sources for studying this topic are inscriptions found on stone tablets. This essay is based on an examination of such inscriptions and makes the following points.

(1) In the sixteenth century, Suzhou was at the center of the most advanced development in industry and commerce. One of its distinctive features is the appearance of numerous native-place associations *(huiguan)* and professional guilds *(gongsuo)*. They were at once a manifestation of a developing commodity economy and a facilitation of industry and commerce in Suzhou.

(2) The inscriptions attest to more than ninety such associations, and there were doubtless many more. The earliest *huiguan* was founded during the Ming Wanli period; their number peaked during the Qing Qianlong period. Such associations can be categorized into seven types: those founded by (a) merchants pooling their resources, (b) handicraft workshops pooling their resources, (c) craftsmen alone, (d) officials, (e) merchants and handicraft workshops jointly, (f) merchants and officials jointly, and (g) natives of the same locality or region.

(3) The *huiguan* or *gongsuo* regulated relationships and increased cooperation within its own trade. Acting as a group, association members sought a competitive advantage. In Suzhou *huiguan* and *gongsuo* all placed great emphasis on relief work, and the greater part of a *huiguan'* s expenditures were typically devoted to medical care, medicine, free private schools, unemployment aid, money for returning home, care of the aged, public cemeteries, and burial costs. Such benevolent actions played their part in the long-term welfare of the particular trade and muted the contradictions between employer and employees.

(4) At the outset, the *huiguan* and *gongsuo* often laid down rules, known as *hanggui*, which governed entry into the trade, apprentices, masters, and so on. However, these controls tended to weaken as the commodity economy developed. Other *gongsuo* had no rules even at their founding, having been formed solely for welfare purposes. Because their traditional forms of control had

weakened, some guilds at the end of the Qing and the beginning of the Republican era naturally evolved into the industrial trade unions of capitalism.

(5) As early as the sixteenth century, the silk industry in Suzhou already manifested the employment relationships of capitalism. Silk workers, who voluntarily exchanged their labor for wages in order to make a living, were precocious proletarians. By the beginning of the Qing, capitalist employment relationships were spreading beyond the silk industry to dyeing, the mercerized cotton industry, paper manufacture, furniture making, and metallurgy. These industries were not small: the mercerized cotton industry at the beginning of the Qing employed more than 10,000 workers, and the paper industry more than 800 in thirty-three firms.

(6) According to stone inscriptions, wages were based on skill and on piecework. An inscription of 1756 preserves twenty-four rules that determined the wage level, taking into account such factors as level of skill and work quota, which shows that the early capitalists of Ming Suzhou already understood the use of incentives. Such a wage system was brought into being by the sprouts of capitalism.

(7) With the growth of these sprouts, new contradictions and struggles emerged. During the late Ming, owners and workers were united against the common enemy of feudal autocratic rule; the urban movements of 1601, led by Ge Cheng, and of 1626, led by Yan Peiwei, are examples of this alliance. But by the early Qing, owners and workers were in opposition, as shown by inscriptions of 1693 and 1734, which describe the suppression of strikes.

(8) In feudal China protocapitalism was nurtured by the development of a commodity economy. Suzhou in the sixteenth century already showed capitalist sprouts in its production relationships. They grew, and the resulting strikes and struggles are a reflection of that growth. However, because the feudal autocracy strangled industry and commerce during the three hundred years that followed, the production relationships of capitalism remained at the sprouting stage.

CHINA'S LANDLORD ECONOMY AND THE SPROUTS OF AGRARIAN CAPITALISM

Li Wenzhi

To understand how agricultural capitalism developed in China we must first consider some special features of feudal landownership. Unlike the manorial landlord economy in the West, China's landlord economy had certain flexible features: free exchange and transfer of land and the absence of any rigid class structure based on land. These features made possible the development of a commercial economy. During the Ming and Qing periods, the feudal social arrangements of ancestor worship and close kinship ties began to change. At the same time, commercialized agriculture developed as various areas began to specialize in growing tobacco, sugarcane, etc. Cash crops brought higher household earnings, and agricultural producers were tied more closely to the market. The development of this commercial economy also fostered social differentiation in the countryside.

These same developments began to alter the old tenant-landlord relationship. During Song and Yuan times the majority of tenants were bound tightly to their locale, but during the Ming and Qing periods their socioeconomic position became increasingly less servile. By the early Qing, permanent tenancy was widespread. The payment of fixed crop rent was more conspicuous than share rent. As the productivity of the land increased, the burden of rental payments gradually decreased, and some tenants were even able to save enough income to become rich peasants and landlords.

As for the agricultural labor force, families that had been locked into feudal bondage became free to sell their labor. Hired laborers gradually gained freedom from their masters and raised their status—changes that were clearly reflected in revisions of the Qing civil code. However, this sort of emancipation was limited to the work force under commoner landlords; it did not extend to the gentry-landlord class.

The appearance of rich peasants by the mid-Ming presaged the managerial commoner landlords of the early Qing. Commoner landlords found it easy to develop more egalitarian relationships with their hired laborers. Although subconsciously they tended to organize their production in accordance with capitalist principles, their exploitation was different from that practiced by gentry landlords, who often had recourse to noneconomic coercive means in controlling their tenants and hired laborers.

The first sprouts of agricultural capitalism appeared in the fifteenth century. Its development was extraordinarily slow-paced, taking some three hundred years to enter a new stage. At no time did the rate of growth accelerate rapidly. The rigidity of the landlord economy was partly responsible for this phenomenon. For example, some managerial landlords who had earlier employed hired labor reverted to leasing their land—a step backward from capitalistic behavior. Some commoner landlords tried various strategies to acquire gentry-landlord status rather than practicing a style of profit-oriented capitalistic management. In this way, regressive forces managed to hold back the natural growth of agricultural capitalism in China.

ON THE FORCES OF THE JIANGNAN
(SOUTH OF THE CHANGJIANG RIVER) GROUP

Li Xun

This essay is divided into three parts. The first describes the special characteristics of the economic structure of Jiangnan during the Ming. The second describes the formation of local group power in the Jiangnan region. The third describes how this group power waxed and waned as part of the dynamic of political struggle during the Ming.

Part 1 of the essay shows that although Jiangnan was still dominated by a feudal economy during the Ming period, it was nonetheless the most productive and most advanced of China's regional economies. Its economic structure was characterized by two special features. First, the autocratic rule of the Ming had made the region the most heavily taxed in all of China. The extremely heavy land tax and corvée duties not only set agricultural producers in opposition to the state but also created a contradiction between the power of Jiangnan landlords and Ming rulers. Second, despite heavy exploitation by the Ming rulers, Jiangnan achieved a high level of economic development. This paradoxical phenomenon was due to the fact that Jiangnan's agriculture, handicraft industries, and commerce had all developed beyond a strictly feudal mode. In addition, certain Ming economic policies had the effect of encouraging economic development. Given the special characteristics of Jiangnan's economic structure, it is clear that local power in Jiangnan was on a collision course with feudal autocracy and that conflict was inevitable. Moreover, only in Jiangnan was collective power great enough to carry out this struggle.

The second section of the essay contends that because of the economic development of the Jiangnan region, and especially because of the unprecedented development of contract labor in the cities, there naturally arose two sorts of divisions based on the mode of production. The first sort was the division of the landowning class into managerial landlords and rich peasant proprietors; the second was the division of small-scale producers into hired laborers and workshop owners on the one hand and commercial capitalists on the other. These divisions yielded four groups: gentry landlords, managerial landlords, great merchants, and handicraft producers consisting of the owners of workshops and their hired laborers. The collective political power of Jiangnan represents the coalescence of these four groups in response to the struggle against aristocratic power. This was a reflection of the special characteristics of the historical stage in which Jiangnan found itself by this period.

The essay's third section distinguishes three stages in the struggle between local power in Jiangnan and the aristocratic landlord class. From the beginning of the Ming through the Zhengtong period, the struggle was characterized by progressive economic conflict. At that time no group representing collective political power had yet appeared. From the Tianshun period to the end of the Jiajing period, both sides made use of collective organizational power. Conflict moved beyond the strictly economic sphere and presaged the fierce political struggle of the late Ming, what is referred to here as the Donglin Party and Restoration Society stage. This period is characterized not only by the intensification of the struggle but also by progressive polarization, as each of the power groups in the Jiangnan region committed itself to a common struggle against the aristocratic landlord class.

Collective political power in Jiangnan during the Ming period represented, among other things, the growing economic and political strength of the region. The struggles that occurred are unavoidable in the later stages of a feudal society. The waxing and waning of the struggle and its final outcome are all relevant to the issue of protocapitalism and its development and frustration in Chinese feudal society. The continued frustration of the development of regional power in Jiangnan influenced the course of economic development not only in Jiangnan itself but also in China as a whole.

PRIVATE SEA TRADE MERCHANTS AND THE *WOKOU*
IN THE MING DYNASTY

Lin Renchuan

This paper is divided into three sections. The first consists of an investigation into the nature and origin of the so-called "Japanese pirates" *(wokou)* who were active on the southeastern coast of China during the mid-sixteenth century. Although a number of Japanese did participate in *wokou* disturbances at this time, the paper points out that the vast majority of those involved, including all of the important *wokou* leaders, were, in fact, Chinese. For this reason, any suggestions that the Ming government's military operations against the *wokou* during the Jiajing reign (1522-1566) constituted some kind of national struggle against foreign invaders can no longer be seriously entertained. The troubles occurring at that time clearly had a great deal more to do with domestic political and economic considerations than with external causes.

Nevertheless, external causes cannot be dismissed entirely, and the paper's second section begins with a brief survey of the important developments in Chinese maritime trade prior to the sixteenth century, focusing in particular on the government's unsuccessful attempts to control that trade for strategic and other reasons. The paper then moves on to a discussion of the spectacular development of private maritime trade which began in the late fifteenth century and burst into flower during the sixteenth. As China's trading links with the outside world expanded, more and more people along the southeastern coast became involved in maritime commerce in order to take advantage of the unprecedented opportunities.

As might be expected, however, these developments did not go unnoticed by the Ming government, which was always concerned about potential foreign threats to its security. It was particularly unhappy about the increasingly close contact between its citizens and traders from Japan, a country with which the dynasty had previously experienced serious difficulties. Nevertheless, trade between the two countries was so important to the residents of China's southeastern coast that when the Ming authorities tried to suppress it, the *wokou* (as they were mistakenly called) reacted with violence. Thus, it can be seen that the primary cause of the "Japanese troubles" *(woluan)* was the anticommercial policy of the Ming government.

Although it cannot be denied that *wokou* activities caused some damage to the mid-Ming economy, their impact was not entirely negative. Indeed, in a very real sense it can be argued that they helped to stimulate economic growth in the southeast of the country. They did so by altering government perceptions of the importance of maritime trade and by fostering changes in the dynasty's system of taxation, both of which facilitated that trade and encouraged the agricultural and industrial production needed to sustain it. In short, there can be little doubt that private maritime trade was an important factor in the emergence of the "sprouts of capitalism" for which the late Ming period is renowned.

SONG LEGAL PRIVILEGES

Brian E. McKnight

In any society some social groups have more political power and privilege than others, and within any particular group some persons have more power and privileges than others. This problem—the differential distribution of power—has attracted the attention of sinologists, but their concern has been focused on mobility into and out of the ruling elite. There has been little effort to assess the varying extent to which subgroups of the elite shared power.

In this paper an attempt is made to provide an index of the distribution of power. The principal thesis of the paper is that, with certain obvious exceptions, the possession of privileges is a good indicator of the possession of power. Even though not all of the privileged were politically powerful, it is true that all of the politically powerful were privileged. A careful examination of the kinds and degrees of privilege accorded different sectors of the elite tells us a good deal about the distribution of power within the elite.

The two most obvious forms of privilege are freedom or relief from fiscal burdens and from the regular functioning of the law. Each type of privilege has, in turn, both a legal and a practical face. This paper is concerned only with legal privileges and, within that narrowed purview, only with their strictly legal dimension. There was insufficient time to study fiscal privileges or the extent to which legally granted exemptions from the law were taken advantage of in actual cases.

After describing the characteristics of the four major legal privileges of Deliberation (yi), Petition (qing), Reduction (jian), and Commutation (shu), all of which were inherited by the Song from the Tang, the paper goes on to describe the distribution of these privileges among the elite. The elite groups considered include members of the imperial family (by blood and by marriage) and groups with official titles, offices, or honors.

An examination of the distribution of privileges among these groups makes it clear that the degree of privilege was closely related to the amount of political power and influence a group member might possess. This examination also reveals a trend during the Song toward tying the bestowal of privileges more closely to the possession of substantively powerful political positions (as opposed to merely honorary titles or offices) and, in general, toward an increase in the privileges of officials. This latter development is reflected most clearly in a law granting officials in each grade the privileges of the next higher grade. It is also reflected in the extension of privileges to some very minor officials and to potential officials. This downward extension was coupled with the withdrawal of privileged status from some purely honorary titles.

One possible conclusion of this study is that during the Song the power position of the bureaucrats increased and that it increased most importantly among the lowest levels of the state apparatus. This change may in turn reflect a weakening of central state control over local governmental affairs.

THE DEVELOPMENT OF THE HANDICRAFT INDUSTRY IN THE FIRST HALF OF THE QING DYNASTY

Peng Zeyi

This essay examines the recovery and development of the Qing handicraft industry (including metalworking) during the seventeenth and eighteenth centuries from the standpoint of the empirewide economy. It uses concrete historical data to explain how early Qing rule promoted productive forces and stimulated socioeconomic development.

Part 1 describes the basic policies of the Qing state toward handicraft workers and the handicraft industry. Of these, four are of major importance. (1) The government abolished the Ming system of hereditary registered craftsmen. In effect, this policy liberated handicraft workers by eliminating their obligation to perform corvée labor. (2) The government altered the tax structure to exclude taxes in kind in silk, satin, or cotton goods. This served to expand market exchange and aided the development of the handicraft textile industry. (3) The government decreased the size and scope of official handicraft industries and began to use hired laborers within these industries. It also eliminated the obligation of civilian handicraft shops and workers in the same industry (e.g., pottery or cotton cloth) to provide goods or services. This lessened exploitation and helped develop production. (4) The government liberalized the operation of civilian mining and the metalworking industry. In general, the state simply collected taxes and did not manage production directly, thus expanding the scope for civilian activities in this area. Not only did the Qing government change the structure and methods of exploitation, it also took steps to eliminate the corruption that had become infamous during the Ming. Although feudal relations and exploitation remained excessive under Qing rule, the measures adopted allowed the direct producers (peasants and handicraft workers) to develop their own economy and helped to stimulate the forces and relations of production.

Part 2 traces the development of mining and industry during the Qing. The recovery and development of mining and industrial production was part of the general recovery and expansion of the empirewide economy after the Ming. It may be seen in terms of four stages: (1) a difficult period of wartime destruction and recovery of production (1644-1683); (2) a period of basic recovery of the feudal economy (1684-1712); (3) a period of rapid expansion and prosperity (1713-1783); and (4) a period of decelerating expansion of the economy (1784-1839). The basic conditions in industry and mining are concretely described for each period, and quantitative data are mustered to illustrate the dominant trends in economic development. In general, it took sixty years for the economy to recover after the wartime destruction. A more or less stabilized economic prosperity was maintained for seventy years. Then, after signs of stagnation for fifty-odd years, the Qing economy began to decline, heading for an increasingly severe crisis.

Part 3 discusses the great advances in production made during the Qing. We may single out for discussion three major aspects of the expansion of mining and industry. (1) The increase in social productive forces, most apparent in metal extraction and metalworking. Developments in these industries indicate that the productive forces of feudal Chinese society entered a new, higher stage of development in the eighteenth century. (2) The expansion of production for trade. In response to the increased amount of goods produced for the market, there was a steady increase in the flow of goods moved by merchants to distant markets. The production of commercial goods and the increased circulation of commodities are prerequisites for capitalism. (3) The transformation in the relations of production. This occurred in response to the development of productive forces. During this period the individualistic operations of handicraft production were increasingly unable to fulfill the demands of the expanding market for manufactured goods. So long as a single worker performed all operations on a product from beginning to end, possibilities for increasing production and lowering prices were limited. To change this situation, it was necessary to make basic changes in the production process, to raise the output of handicraft workers, and to increase output. Therefore, many merchants moved from merely organizing small-scale producers to distributing products and organizing large-scale retail operations.

To take the analysis one step further, during the eighteenth century merchant capital became industrial capital and accelerated the formative process whereby Chinese feudal society gave birth to the earliest capitalist industrial and mining concerns. During the 1720s and 1730s, in such fields as mining, salt production, lumber processing, paper making, and tea and sugar processing, the production sector gave rise to many large-scale plants and handicraft factories. Clearly, the Qing period witnessed a giant step forward in the development of the forces and relations of production.

The Qing handicraft industry gave rise to several protocapitalist concerns, which must be seen as new elements in the economy. Although these protocapitalist economic elements were nurtured in the womb of feudal society by new forces of production, the new relationships of production they represented did not grow to maturity. Thus, Qing developments did not lead to any profound change in the existing system.

THE FORM OF LAND RENT
AND ITS EVOLUTION DURING THE SONG DYNASTY

Qi Xia

Significant changes took place in China's feudal society during the Song, and these changes were inevitably reflected in the nature of land rents. Rent was an important means by which the 6 or 7 percent of the population that made up the landlord class exploited the masses of landless peasants as well as the lowest level of owner-cultivators. Each type of land rent had a distinctive effect upon agriculture—some hindered and others stimulated output.

Regional variations were marked. In relatively backward areas, such as Chuanxia circuit, one still found estates farmed by serfs, and labor rent remained as one means for appropriating surpluses. But in more developed regions, rent was commonly paid in kind according to a predetermined share between landlord and tenant—ranging from 30-70 to 60-40, with 50-50 the most prevalent. In some of the areas where production was highly developed, for example, the circuits of Liangjiang and Jiangdong, a fixed-rent system evolved that included money rent as well as rent in kind.

Land rents rose steadily throughout the Song period, and by the middle of the Southern Song every kind of rent constituted a heavy burden on the masses of peasants. The era of labor rent was over, and its traces in some areas only hindered agricultural production. In regions where sharecropping left 50 percent or more of the output to the tenant-farmer, he generally put forth every effort to increase output. But the annexation of land by large landlords, combined with population growth and a decline in available land for the tenant farmer, made sharecropping an obstacle to expanded production. Fixed rents were a response to the increase in productivity; they lent impetus to the refinement of farming techniques in Liangjiang and similarly advanced areas and thereby raised yields. Agricultural production in these areas developed at a rapid rate. The emergence of money rent in China antedated that in Europe by two or three centuries.

The sale of land was an important method whereby landownership became more and more concentrated during the Song. As rents rose, so did the price of land. During the Southern Song, the price of land was closely tied to rent.

Where the land rent was high, the value of the land was high; where it was low, the value was low; and when rent fell, the price of land also fell. Land sales in Song China are to be distinguished from those in a strictly capitalist society, primarily because political power often intruded, sometimes to the point where the state made forcible purchases of good land. Nonetheless, land was bought and sold during the Song with its value fixed by rents.

Do these facts show that within the feudal society of Song China changes were taking place that presaged the emergence of sprouts of agricultural capitalism? This question awaits further study.

EDUCATION, FUNCTIONAL LITERACY, AND
THEIR ECONOMIC AND SOCIAL EFFECTS

Evelyn S. Rawski

This essay is divided into three parts. Part 1 discusses distinctions in levels of literacy and briefly surveys the historical development of literacy in China. Major factors stimulating expansion of functional literacy in Ming-Qing times include the adoption of education as the dominant mode of bureaucratic recruitment, increases in the supply of teachers, expansion of educational facilities, expansion of printing, and the rising demand for literacy skills in the economy and society.

Part 2 reviews the social science literature on the historical role of literacy in promoting industrializaion. The English case and other recent writings emphasize the role of attitudinal and behavioral transformations rather than literacy per se. Analysis of Japanese modernization also supports the contention that the content of premodern education was less important than the role of the educational system in promoting positive attitudes toward knowledge, extending the recruitment of talent, promoting social mobility, and inculcating the populace with rule through the written word.

Part 3 surveys recent trends in social history in the West: demographic research, the new English legal history, study of material culture, medical history, popular religious history, and the study of mentalities. Scholars in these disparate subjects share a willingness to seek new data, use quantitative methods in the analysis of data, and structure their research with social science concepts and methods. Their work provides the Chinese historian with a comparative perspective and a variety of topics and methods that might advance the quest for a better understanding of China's past.

HISTORICAL DEMOGRAPHY: SOURCES AND INDICATORS FOR THE STUDY OF THE QING POPULATION

Gilbert Rozman

In recent years historical demography has transformed many areas of research (e.g., economic history, urban history, history of social classes, and family history), and its impact is likely to be no less profound on Chinese studies than it has been on European and Japanese studies. Nevertheless, despite some attempts by specialists on premodern China to take population variables into account, there is little awareness of what data are available even for the Qing, the best documented of the dynastic periods.

This paper reviews seven types of population records and recent efforts to use them: (1) statistics for administrative units recorded in gazetteers (fang-zhi), (2) data on the distribution of ages, (3) population information on villages, clusters of villages, and cities (often in little-used sources such as the Jinmen baojia tushuo [Explanation for the baojia maps of Tianjin county] of 1846 and the Qing xian cuntu [Village maps of Qing county] of 1877), (4) household records (huce), (5) genealogical records (jiapu), (6) modern census records compiled in Taiwan and the Guandong peninsula of Manchuria when these areas were under Japanese occupation, and (7) survey research such as John Lossing Buck's land-utilization study of 1929-1931. It is questionable whether any of these records adequately meets scholarly needs for a reassessment of Qing population; yet collectively they offer a wide variety of useful information.

Available data have been used to estimate variations in sex ratio, age distribution, mean household size, and the rate of population growth. Within North China the geographical distribution of several of these variables has been analyzed and explanations suggested for observed relationships among vari-ables. A typology of urban areas has been proposed based on demographic indicators. The data have also been examined to determine the extent to which the presence of particular social strata is associated with particular ranges in mean household size and age distribution. Reanalysis of Buck's survey data shows a population with high mortality and surprisingly low marital fertility.

In conclusion, the paper draws certain comparisons with Japan, tentatively suggesting sharp contrasts between demographic changes in the two countries, and assesses the quality of materials on Qing population and the main findings to date.

MARKETING SYSTEMS AND REGIONAL ECONOMIES:
THEIR STRUCTURE AND DEVELOPMENT

G. William Skinner

The objectives of this paper are to demonstrate the utility of regional systems theory for historical analysis and to analyze the internal structure and historical development of regional economies during the middle and late imperial eras.

The paper decries the overreliance of most economic historians on provinces, prefectures, and counties as units of analysis, arguing that the distribution of production factors, the forces and relations of production, and all aspects of marketing and trade were shaped and constrained primarily by the hierarchy of economic central places (as opposed to administrative central places, i.e., capitals) and of associated local and regional economic systems (i.e., commercial hinterlands as opposed to administrative units). Basic-level market towns, of which there were some 27,000 in late Qing times, were but the bottom rung of a hierarchy of economic central places that had seven or eight levels, depending on the region. Place in this hierarchy was associated with economic function. Centers at any given level were distinguished from those at the next lower level by the presence of (or greater number of) firms offering more specialized goods and services. In general, as one ascended the hierarchy, commerce, industry, credit, storage, and transport were increasingly differentiated from one another, and within each of these functional spheres, occupational differentiation, product specialization, and institutionalization steadily increased. Economic centers at each ascending level served as the nodes of ever more extensive and complex territorial economic systems. Such systems at any one level were articulated with more inclusive systems through a complex network in which one center might be oriented to one, two, or three centers at the next higher level. A significant feature of the overall structure was that systems at each higher level overlapped a number of systems at the next lower level and completely enveloped several systems at the level below that.

The hierarchy of nested economic systems was sharply constrained by the structure of river systems, topography, and other physiographic givens.

According to the analysis presented, the hierarchical structure of ever more inclusive economic systems culminated in some twenty-six metropolitan trading systems, many of whose limits were defined by mountain barriers, and these in turn formed eight great economic systems, each essentially coterminous with one of China's physiographic macroregions. The paper analyzes in detail the internal structure of the Upper Yangzi regional economy and briefly describes the structure of two others. Each macroregional system is shown to be characterized by the concentration of resources of all kinds—arable land, population, capital investments—in a central area and a thinning out of resources toward the periphery. Apart from the special case of Yungui, macroregional cores corresponded to river valley lowlands, which almost by definition enjoyed higher levels of agricultural productivity and critical transport advantages. As a consequence, the major cities of each region grew up in the core area, and the various cities within a macroregional system developed hierarchical patterns climaxing in one or more core cities. Transactions between the centrally located cities of one region and those of another were minimized by the high cost of unmechanized transport and the great distances involved. Significant interregional trade was limited to the water routes linking the Lower Yangzi region with its immediate neighbors. At the opposite extreme from the relatively open, urbanized economy of the Lower Yangzi were the autarkic and underurbanized economies of Yungui and the Upper Yangzi. While holding level in the hierarchy of constant marketing systems, the paper documents systematic variation in the characteristics of marketing and trading systems according to place in the core-periphery structure of macroregional systems—such characteristics as population size (of the system and of its node), demand density, and degree of competition.

Regional systems analysis takes a functional approach to the temporal as well as the spatial aspects of human interaction—and, indeed, views the two as inseparable. It is argued that the temporal patterns of which human history is ultimately constructed are properties of systems of human interaction, territorial systems included. Thus, regional economies and their lower-order component systems have characteristic rhythms and distinctive histories. The point is illustrated for basic-level marketing systems, but major attention is focused at the macroregional level. The thesis here is that the economic development, demographic history, and sociopolitical dynamics of each macroregional system have displayed a long-term cyclical rhythm, and that the cycles of different macroregional systems were seldom closely synchronized. The argument is carried forward through a comparison of successive developmental cycles in North China and the Southeast Coast. An analysis is then made of the various factors favoring the synchronization of regional developmental cycles and of the often more decisive factors opposing it. It is argued in particular that, in its impact on the economy, the dynastic cycle was mediated by regional developmental cycles.

Two methodological morals may be drawn from the theoretical emphasis on spatial-cum-temporal systems. If historical/temporal patterns are indeed systematic, then they may be reliably identified—in fact, they are likely to emerge with clarity—only when the analysis is focused on or specified for the pertinent system. Moreover, no finding concerning secular trends is valid unless the data have been analytically controlled for phase in the cycles intrinsic to the relevant system.

THE RISE AND FALL OF THE SALT MERCHANTS ALONG
THE HUAIHE RIVER DURING THE FIRST HALF OF THE QING DYNASTY

Wang Sizhi and Jin Chengji

Salt taxes constituted a large part of Qing revenues. It was said that the yearly taxes in the Liang-Huai salt region made up half of the entire empire's salt taxes and that state plans depended heavily on their payment. Hence, the salt merchants of Liang-Huai occupied an extremely important position in the economic life of China. The history of their rise and fall reflects the prosperity and decline of the Qing court.

During the wars that marked the transition from the Ming to the Qing, one after another of the salt merchants of Liang-Huai went bankrupt. Although the Qing declared a policy of "relief to merchants and lightening of taxes," this policy was not fully enforced so long as fighting continued. Throughout the Shunzhi reign, the salt merchants of Liang-Huai faced difficult times. After complete pacification in the 1680s, however, the Qing policy of "relief to merchants and lightening of taxes" was carried out more seriously. Under the protection of salt administrators and the emperor, the Liang-Huai salt merchants developed rapidly.

The Qing continued the Ming salt laws with some adaptations. They put into effect the *gangyin* system based on official supervision and merchant management. The Liang-Huai salt merchants were mainly transport merchants. Among them, the *zongshang*, or head merchants, who were the effective monopolists of the salt industry, represented all the merchants in their dealings with the Qing salt administration. The opinions of the *zongshang* frequently influenced Qing salt policies, even to the point of overturning imperial decisions. Certain regulations of the Qing government benefited the salt merchants. Notable among these were: (1) the system whereby salt factories operated depots, ensuring that salt merchants had a monopoly on salt production; (2) the division of areas in which salt was sold, guaranteeing monopolies for the salt merchants in the ports of distribution; and (3) the protection of salt merchants through pricing policies. These policies were adopted in order to guarantee salt revenues. But because salt merchants monopolized production and marketing and could raise prices at will, they obtained very high profits. In addition, there was some recourse to dishonest tactics such as smuggling and tax evasion. With accelerating population growth, salt sales boomed. As a result, by the Qianlong period, Liang-Huai salt merchants had become a feudalist bloc owning monopolistic commercial capital of tens of millions. The head merchants among them in turn formed a financial clique in the early Qing.

This bloc, whether private or official, had inextricably close ties to the Qing government. Not only did several million dollars of salt taxes go into the state storehouse each year, but the imperial family's lavish outlays and the Imperial Household Department's revenues derived largely from salt profits and the private means of salt merchants. The relationship between salt officials and salt merchants truly was "officials get rich through exploiting merchants; merchants gain protection through feeding officials." Every time the viceroy advocated controlling the price of salt, salt officials strenuously opposed it. Salt officials were allied with salt merchants in opposition to the viceroy and the Ministry of Finance.

Beginning in the late Qianlong period, and especially from the Jiaqing period, the salt merchants of Liang-Huai began to go into decline. They were seen as "something which can be eaten." From Qianlong to Jiaqing, each contribution could be reckoned in the tens of millions. On top of that, miscellaneous fees were added to the regular taxes and constantly increased.

Suppression of the White Lotus Rebellion, which exploded in five provinces from 1796 to 1804, required one hundred million taels of silver. Thus, even more was demanded of the salt merchants. The burden proved too heavy for them. Moreover, their own extravagance was amazing to behold. All these demands were added to the cost of salt, so the price rose unabated. With official prices so high, private salt flooded the market. Salt merchants were on the brink of bankruptcy. Salt laws broke down. Because of this, the governor-general of Liang-Jiang, Tao Zhu, instituted reforms during the Daoguang reign. Tao replaced the *gangyin* system with the *piaofa* (ticket) system in order to counter smuggling. Even small merchants with little capital were permitted to ship goods if they could pay the taxes. Thus was the monopoly of the Liang-Huai merchants broken. Following the abolition of the *gangyin* system, most of the *zongshang* disappeared without a trace.

THE SECULAR MOVEMENT OF GRAIN PRICES IN CHINA, CA. 1760-1910

Yeh-chien Wang

In an agrarian society, food supply is crucial to the maintenance of economic, social, and political stability. For this reason the successive dynasties in China all considered it a major responsibility of the state to maintain adequate supplies of grain throughout the empire. The Manchu government set up a unique grain price reporting system to monitor the grain supply in all parts of the country. Under this system each governor and governor-general was required to submit to the emperor a monthly report of the prices of principal grains in every prefecture of the province under his jurisdiction. Numerous reports of this kind are preserved at the National Palace Museum in Taibei; they contain rich data for observing price changes, temporally and geographically, in late imperial China.

This paper investigates the long-term trend of grain prices during the latter half of the Qing period. From the price data collected from the above-mentioned reports, I have selected for analysis the data on rice and wheat for five major prefectures in southeastern China—Suzhou, Jiangning, Hangzhou, Anqing, and Fuzhou. Excluding the period from the 1760s through the early 1770s and the greater part of the 1850s and 1860s, for which data are insufficient or completely lacking, we find that in all five prefectures grain prices move in two long waves. One wave ascends from the 1780s to a peak in the mid-1830s and then descends to a trough in 1853. When the data resume in 1870 the trend is downward, reaching a trough in the early 1880s, after which prices rise to an unprecedented height near the end of the Qing period.

Grain was the most important commodity on the market in agrarian China, and changes in its prices led to price changes for most other commodities. Grain prices, then, were unquestionably the leading indicator of general prices. The level of general prices is determined by the quantity of money in circulation and the quantity of goods and services available in the market. Thus, we may interpret the secular movement of grain prices during this period in terms of changes in two variables—money and goods. The upswing phase of both waves is explained by the fact that the supply of money expanded at a greater rate than did the supply of goods in the market, for in both periods

(1780–early 1830s and 1880–1910) China witnessed a simultaneous and remarkable increase in three kinds of circulating media—silver, copper coins, and paper notes. The downswing in the first wave was clearly brought about by the sharp contraction in the money supply that followed the rise of the opium trade in the second quarter of the nineteenth century. The downswing in the second wave resulted mainly from the restoration of production and trade following nearly a quarter-century of social upheaval.

THE SOCIAL STATUS OF PEASANTS IN CHINESE HISTORY

Wang Yuquan

The correct understanding of peasant status is a fundamental issue in the historiography of ancient China. The few analyses that exist hold that peasants in ancient China were "owner-cultivators," that is, "free and independent" self-cultivators. These phrases refer to the mode of management, but they also imply status. If we looked at this issue superficially, we could easily confuse the peasant in ancient China with his counterpart in eighteenth-century Europe, who managed his own farm and had a free and independent status. Would it be correct to characterize the peasant in ancient China in such terms?

What the studies refer to, of course, are households outside the category of tenants. There is no reliable procedure for estimating the proportion of tenants vis-à-vis owner-cultivators in ancient times, and that proportion would be expected to vary in time and space. In a strong dynasty, free cultivators could outnumber tenants. Generally speaking, owner-cultivators were more numerous in northern China, and tenants more numerous in the south. If the number of agricultural producers who were "free and independent" was indeed large, we could hardly refer to ancient China as a feudal society. But how could these "freeholders" exist in a feudal society? The correct answer to this question provides a key to understanding ancient Chinese history.

In a feudal society the rulers and the ruled form two opposing classes. Despite some turnover of personnel, the ruling class in China maintained unbroken continuity. Officials and commoners were treated very differently. The land of the great landlords was not taxed, while that of the commoners was. Another major sign of status was whether or not one was subject to the corvée. Members of the imperial household and high officials were exempt from corvée, while commoners in general were not.

We must also consider government control. Households had to register with the government. They were then organized into mutual security groups of five and ten. Nor could households move about freely—if they did move, they would again be forced to register. This system of control lasted for two or three thousand years. Are we dealing during these millennia with a "free" peasantry?

The notion that the land tax was more onerous than the corvée does not accord with the historical reality of ancient China. The corvée was much heavier. Households and *ding* were basic units of taxation. The status of those who were taxed and those who taxed was very different. This kind of supraeconomic coercion resulted in a variety of unfree relationships.

Assignment of households to corvée service was probably an ancient tradition, although its early forms are not clear. The system that survived into the Ming period began to take shape during the Nan-Bei dynasties. Households were registered for different duties. In this system, ordinary civilian households were the most numerous. Military households were next, then artisans. Today we find it hard to imagine such a hereditary system, where people could not shift from one household category to another. That households had to fulfill these services shows that they were neither free nor independent. Moreover, the emperor could bestow tenant households on lords. That is, he could transform owner-cultivators into tenants. This suggests how "free" peasants were in ancient China.

"Freehold" is a European term the Chinese do not use, although we do have a similar concept. Free transactions in land have been taken as proof of the existence of landownership rights. Can this linkage be assumed? In order for the populace to perform corvée duties, the Zhou kings and subsequent emperors had to give them some land to support themselves. The state combined the land tax with corvée labor in what proved to be a successful strategy for the ruling elite. When land became alienable, the labor-tax burden on that land was transferred as well. Because the land carried with it corvée and feudal services, one cannot easily see it as "freehold" property. With corvée obligations attached to land, can one properly consider land transactions to be free?

The feudal authoritarian state was neither profit-seeking nor development-oriented but rather a conservative closed economy with an antimercantile policy. Nonetheless, dynamic economic elements did emerge. Commerce, which developed in the Tang and Song, infiltrated and altered the feudal authoritarian economic base. There were changes in the tax system and in social relationships. It was not politics but commerce and production for trade that opened up the closed natural economy, destroyed the antimercantile policy, broke up the feudal classes, and raised the social status of the merchant. Commerce and production for trade altered the respective positions of the building blocks of the economy: households (labor power) and land (productive resource). By the Ming period, households no longer played as important a role as land in the feudal economy. Nevertheless, the basic structure of the feudal economy persisted; commercial development did not alter its essence.

To sum up, the status of peasants in ancient China was by no means free and independent. Peasants belonged to the emperor. Commoners probably never entertained ideas of freedom and independence. In ancient Chinese political thought the concept of human rights was unknown.

SOME PROBLEMS CONCERNING *JIAOZI* IN THE NORTHERN SONG PERIOD

Wang Zengyu

The *jiaozi* (exchange medium) of the Northern Song was the earliest paper currency in history. Both Chinese and foreign scholars have already made many contributions to the study of this form of money. In building on these earlier investigations, this essay focuses on three questions.

First, what were the preconditions for the use of *jiaozi*? The paper shows that Song China issued the world's earliest paper currency because both the technological and economic prerequisites were present; in particular, one must note the expansion and improvement of woodblock printing and the growth of a money economy. The demand for money had increased sharply, out of all proportion to the supply of bronze coins *(tongqian)* in circulation. Between the Tang and the Song, *duanbai* (short strings), *tieqian* (iron coins), and deposit notes were all used to supplement bronze coins in areas where their supply was inadequate. In the Sichuan area, iron coins were commonly used, but only at great inconvenience because of their great weight and low value. Thus, the introduction of *jiaozi* was both necessary and inevitable.

Second, what were the limits of the *jie* (period of circulation) of each *jiaozi* issue? In the Northern Song, the *jiaozi* were issued for limited periods of circulation, after which they were redeemed for new notes. The famous Japanese scholar Katō Shigeshi has argued that the *jie* was a period of three years. He interpreted at face value texts stating that "three years constituted a *jie*." In fact, two years constituted a *jie*, but these two years spanned three different calendar years. During the Song, state-managed *jiaozi* were issued from 1023 to 1105, a total of 42 periods of circulation. Even after 1107, when the name was changed to *qianyin* (money voucher), the period of circulation was maintained. However, in the earlier period (1011-1023), when *jiaozi* were privately issued by merchants, one period of circulation lasted approximately three full years.

Third, did the purchasing power of *jiaozi* remain relatively stable? I argue that during the first fifty years of its history as a government money, *jiaozi* maintained a stable value because the size of issues was based on the supply of iron coins and the quantity issued was strictly controlled. When later in the eleventh century the period of circulation was increased from two to four years, the value of *jiaozi* began to fall, but the rate of decline was still less than 10 percent. It was only after 1094, when the Song court began printing *jiaozi* recklessly, that these notes became practically worthless. Nevertheless, when compared with paper currencies issued during the Southern Song or with those of the Yuan and Ming dynasties, the *jiaozi* of Northern Song must be counted a success.

Appended to the article is a table of "Officially Issued *Jiaozi* of the Northern Song," listing the year of issue, the period of circulation, the quantity printed, and the face value of the notes during each period of circulation.

THE RISE AND FALL OF FAN:
THE NOTED QING IMPERIAL MERCHANT FAMILY

Wei Qingyuan and Wu Qiyan

During the Qing dynasty what have come to be known as "imperial merchants" (huangshang) were granted significant economic and political privileges by the imperial family and carried out commercial operations of great importance for the finances, military needs, and economic life of the feudal court. With a trading network extending from Japan to the northwestern frontier, and with enormous capital at their disposal, these merchants occupied a very important position in the history of Qing commerce.

Among the most influential of the imperial merchants in early Qing times were the famous Fans of Shanxi province, a family which had been economically and politically prominent long before the Manchu conquest of China. Because the Fans had both financial resources and managerial expertise, and because they were already well known to the Manchu leadership, they were summoned to Beijing to become imperial merchants soon after the Qing armies had entered China to stay in 1644.

As the first part of this paper explains, during the early years of the dynasty the Fans used their privileged position as imperial merchants to expand their already wide-ranging operations into many of the most lucrative areas of Qing economic life. From the beginning of the dynasty to the Qianlong reign (1736-1796), for example, the Fans were the most important copper and salt merchants in China. At the same time, they acquired significant political power—their work for the feudal court gained them notice and favor and resulted in some members of the family being appointed to important official positions. Still others achieved success in the civil-service examinations.

If the Fans' close relationship with the court proved beneficial during the early years of the dynasty, however, it also helped to bring about the family's ruin during the late Qianlong reign. There appear to have been several reasons for this. First, although the imperial merchants received many favors and privileges, they were also exploited by the emperor and by his officials. As corruption and greed at all levels of Qing government increased during the late eighteenth century, the exploitation of the Fans and other imperial merchants grew ever more intense. Second, the strict regulation of the economy by the feudal leadership at court severely limited the merchants' freedom and made it difficult for them to invest their capital in new ventures. This eventually undermined their economic position and helped make bankruptcies for many inevitable.

By studying the rise and fall of the Fan family, one can clearly see the restraints which were often placed on commercial capital in feudal society. Much of the enormous wealth accumulated by the Fans and other imperial merchants flowed into imperial storehouses or into the hands of corrupt officials of all ranks. As might be expected, this seriously affected the development of China's feudal economy and hindered the maturation of the "sprouts of capitalism."

THE OPIUM WAR AND CHINA'S TRADE
WITH THE WESTERN COUNTRIES, 1840-1860

Yan Zhongping

After the Opium War, Britain parlayed its military superiority into a position of political superiority to the Qing government. Having suffered defeat at the hands of the British, the Qing government then fell before other Western countries. Thus began the period of indirect political control of China by foreign powers. This kind of control did not rest simply on the so-called "domineering" conduct of the Westerners, but on Western gunboats as well. China's history, whether political, economic, military, or cultural, should be studied with this semicolonial situation clearly in mind.

It was only after the Peking treaties of 1860 that the Qing government, overimpressed by everything foreign, actively gave directives in its own name on behalf of foreign aggression. Prior to that, the government's course was one of passive acquiescence the West. During the 1840s and 1850s, foreign power stood forward on the stage of history, distinguishing itself with extraordinary vigor.

In the series of treaties and agreements between China and Britain that followed the Opium War, not a word was mentioned about opium smuggling or the opium trade. The treaties set out the system to be used by the consuls to control the ports, forcibly removing from the Chinese Customs its power to obtain import and export duties directly from foreign merchants. The treaties stipulated that the British consul had responsibility for "guaranteeing" the Chinese their customs duties. The treaties China signed with the other countries all specified that the consuls were to control the ports, but they failed to stipulate that they were to guarantee customs duties. The system whereby the consuls were to control the ports opened wide a convenient door for foreign merchants to smuggle and avoid paying duties.

In the fourth and fifth decades of the nineteenth century, most of the Western consuls in China were merchants. Thus, Western merchants were in the powerful position of being able to pocket the very customs duties generated through their control of the ports. At that time most Westerners in China were adventurers. Under the protection of Western warships, they turned every place they went into an "adventurer's paradise," smuggling opium, engaging in slave trade, avoiding taxes, killing people—there was nothing they did not do. Previous historians who have explained this rampage of smuggling and tax evasion in terms of the greed and corruption of Chinese officials have not adequately grasped this pivotal point in modern history.

A PRELIMINARY STUDY OF THE UNOFFICIAL LAND SALES IN NORTHERN FUJIAN DURING THE QING DYNASTY

Yang Guozhen

The buying and selling of land is a key characteristic of Chinese feudal society. During the Ming and Qing, private landownership and commercial development led to widespread land transactions. Buying and selling became the major mode of transferring land rights. This essay examines the effect of land sales upon landownership in northern Fujian during the Qing. Three problems are treated.

Land Sales and Divided Ownership Rights. During Qing times, land rights in northern Fujian were generally divided into subsurface and surface rights. Subsurface rights were variously termed "big sprout," "big rent," "crop land," and "bone land"; the corresponding terms for surface rights were "small sprout," "small rent," "tax land," and "skin land." The two kinds of land rights were normally held by different persons. Each was free to dispose of his part and to put his rights up for sale independently. Furthermore, during the progress from an ordinary sale to an absolutely final sale (but excluding the cases where absolute sales were consummated at the first transaction), either party might declare the land a living property, thereby preserving in fact or in intent some ownership rights. Transactions included four stages, and in each stage a contract was drawn up and specific ownership rights were sold off individually until "the heart stops and the bones are broken." This kind of land transaction served to encourage the fragmentation of ownership rights and to keep the transfer of land in a state of flux. The feudal ownership system was ambiguously adaptive, and so tenacious that it was difficult to do away with.

The Silver Owner in Land Transactions. The term "silver owner" *(yinzhu)* became associated with land transactions in the mid-Ming. From an analysis of more than a hundred Qing cases of silver owners in land-sale documents in northern Fujian, it appears that the term refers, not to any specific social class or social stratum, but rather to buyers who paid for ownership rights in cash (silver). Silver owners included landlords, bureaucrats, and merchants as well as self-cultivators and rich peasants. The appearance of silver owners suggests a weakening of feudal political privileges—appropriating land by political

129

means—and is therefore indicative of a loosening of the feudal bonds of society. However, since the commodity economy and protocapitalism were relatively underdeveloped in northern Fujian, the silver owners of that area did not develop into managerial landlords or "rental agricultural capitalists." After the Opium War, some silver owners ventured into industry and commerce while retaining their characteristics as landlords, old-style rich peasants, or secondary landlords (er dizhu). They became an obstacle to change in productive relationships within the village economy.

The Sale of Skin Land and Permanent Tenancy Rights. Permanent tenancy could be purchased. When ownership is divided, tenancy refers to the surface rights, which include the right to farm the land. Once surface rights became objects of sale, they tended to fall into the hands of *peizhu*, i.e., secondary or tertiary landlords. Surface rights were much less commonly purchased by tenant farmers or the owners of "bone land" (those owning subsurface rights). Thus, repeated transactions often gave rise to multiple landownership—"one plot with two owners" or "one plot with three owners." It was the *peizhu* who obtained the greatest benefit from these transactions.

Case studies of land transactions in northern Fujian in Qing times clearly indicate that frequent and widespread land sales did not result in the destruction of feudal landownership rights. On the contrary, by adopting new forms, feudalism was able to consolidate its controlling position in northern Fujian villages. On the eve of the land-reform movement, that region was still poor and underdeveloped, and the feudal landownership system must be seen as part of the cause.

A REPORT ON THE INVESTIGATION OF THE TENANT SYSTEM IN CHAWAN VILLAGE, QIMEN COUNTY, AND MINGZHOU VILLAGE, XIUNING COUNTY, OF HUIZHOU

Ye Xian'en

This essay is based primarily on field surveys and secondarily on documents. It introduces the servile tenancy system that survived to the 1940s in two villages, Chawan and Mingzhou, and advances views on several related problems.

Part 1 surveys the system of servile tenancy in Chawan, Qimen county. The chief characteristic of land tenure in Chawan is that the largest landowner was a corporate lineage. Lineage property tends to increase along with the development of lineage power. Lineage power, usually involving strict control of peasants by landlords, developed as powerful noble families disappeared from the historical stage. The Wang lineage in Chawan dates back to the Southern Song. A lineage hall and elaborate lineage ritual reinforced its organizational unity and strength. From the Zhengde reign (1506-1521) of the Ming until the early Qing, the Wang lineage produced officials in every generation. It began to decline in the mid-Qing. Prominent members used their power within the lineage to control lesser members, a system that culminated in the oppression and enslavement of field servants (dianpu). The essay treats the origins, distribution, terminology, labor duties, and exploitation of field servants in pre-Liberation Chawan. It traces their origins as household slaves and servants, bankrupt peasants who chose submission, and descendants of families expelled from the lineage. An analysis of the distribution of field servant residences shows their relation to topography, the location of cultivated lands, and the requirements of managing mountain fields and corvée labor. The names used for different types of field servants were based on their respective duties. Their rents were comparable to those paid by ordinary tenants, but their labor duties were higher. They owed service to landlords, especially in connection with weddings, funerals, and other ritual occasions.

Part 2 surveys the system of servile tenancy in Mingzhou, Xiuning county. The founders of the Wu lineage entered this area in the Yuan dynasty. Lineage prosperity was based primarily on tea, lumber, and commerce. Although it never produced prominent officials, the lineage diligently fostered the ancestral cult and strictly observed family and lineage rules. There were three types of landownership in the Wu lineage: ownership by particular lineage halls, by the lineage as a whole, and by private families. But the field servants of lineage branch halls and of private families also were the servants of the entire lineage. The essay examines the social status and exploitation of the Wu lineage's field servants in pre-Liberation Mingzhou. On the basis of survey materials, it shows that the phrase "forcing a slave to engage in commerce" mentioned in the literature on Huizhou merchants also applied to field servants.

Part 3 advances views on several questions raised by the survey materials. Most servile dependents were characterized as "farming the owner's land, living in the owner's house, and being buried in the owner's cemetery." Since the key element here is "farming the owner's land," I have used *dianpu* (field servants) as the generic term. Servile tenancy existed alongside the village land system and the labor corvée system. The three influenced one another. Field servants belonged to the declassed social stratum. They were included in the legal category "slaves and servants." Field servants were not the same as slaves, but the historical literature classes them together. In fact, the great majority of producers referred to in the literature on late Ming as "slaves and servants" were field servants. The servile tenancy system slowly eroded from the mid-Qing on. Between 1727 and 1825, Qing rulers issued five edicts to emancipate these people, but the imperial orders ran up against lineage power. Indeed, some of the repealed legal provisions that had compelled peasants to become field servants were retained in family and lineage rules. The local power of lineages and customary lineage law served to bind field servants to their oppressors. This remnant of serfdom survived in Huizhou until Liberation.

PART III:
"THE SINO-AMERICAN SYMPOSIUM ON
CHINESE SOCIOECONOMIC HISTORY
FROM THE SONG DYNASTY TO 1900"

THE SINO-AMERICAN SYMPOSIUM ON
CHINESE SOCIOECONOMIC HISTORY
FROM THE SONG DYNASTY TO 1900

Special to the English Edition
of *Social Sciences in China**

The Sino-American Symposium on Chinese Socioeconomic History from the Song Dynasty to 1900 was held in Beijing from 26 October to 1 November 1980. The symposium was organized as part of the 1980 exchange program between the Chinese Academy of Social Sciences (CASS) and the United States [National] Academy of Sciences Committee on Scholarly Communication with the People's Republic of China. The Chinese delegation of twenty members and ten auditors was headed by Professor Yan Zhongping, Vice-Director of the Institute of Economics under the CASS, Professor Deng Guangming of the Department of History, Beijing University, and Professor Wang Yuquan of the Institute of History under the CASS. The American delegation of ten members and four auditors was led by Professor Albert Feuerwerker, Director of the Center for Chinese Studies, University of Michigan, and Professor G. William Skinner, anthropologist at Stanford University. Noted Chinese scholars Chen Zhenhan, Shen Congwen, Yang Xiangkui, and Xie Guozhen attended as special guest participants. Mr. John Jamieson, academic advisor to the U.S. Embassy in Beijing, was also present.

The thirty-three papers presented to the symposium were the result of years of meticulous and energetic scholarship. They covered a wide range of economic, political, military, cultural, and foreign trade problems of the Song, Ming, and Qing dynasties. The format for the symposium was lively: each author first gave a brief synopsis of his paper, followed by comments and criticisms from a principal commentator and then free discussion. The atmosphere was one of serious academic exploration and lively discussion. The following is an outline of the major problems raised at the symposium.

---

* *Editor's Note: Some minor stylistic changes have been made in the article so that it conforms more closely to the style used in the remainder of this volume. Otherwise, the article has been reprinted as it originally appeared in* Social Sciences in China, no. 1 (1981), pp. 170-94.

135

1. Problems Concerning Rural Society and Economy
and the Social Status of the Peasants

Agriculture has been the foundation of Chinese society since ancient times; it has been the dominant economic sector and peasants have made up the great majority of the population. During the Song, Ming, and Qing dynasties, all social changes were rooted in agriculture. Research into rural society and the condition of peasants, therefore, has been a major topic in the study of this period of Chinese history and a topic that has attracted considerable attention of Chinese and American historians. In "The Social Status of Peasants in Chinese History," Professor Wang Yuquan of the Institute of History, CASS, gave an overall description of the social status of peasants going as far back as the Zhou (ca. eleventh century B.C.-771 B.C.) and Qin (221 B.C.-206 B.C.) dynasties and up to the Ming and Qing dynasties. He challenged the conventional notion held by some scholars both at home and abroad that the Chinese peasants during the feudal period were "free and independent," saying that in a society where "human beings could possess other human beings" and the common people were bound by a census register, there was no such thing as a free and independent peasantry. Neither did the concept exist. Like other human beings under census register, peasants were the property of the emperors. "The emperor was empowered to enslave, exert taxes on, transfer or fix to a place the living bodies of the peasants," Professor Wang said. And "such powers enjoyed by the emperors had never been challenged until the seventeenth century. Neither had it ever been argued as to whether or not it was right for the people under census register to be at the disposal of such powers."

As a commentator on Professor Wang's article, Evelyn S. Rawski, Associate Professor of History at the University of Pittsburgh, said that Wang "has put forward an important question that should be borne in mind. And that is, any effort in the interpretation of history by current ideas would be a distortion of history." She pointed out, however, that during the period of the Ming and Qing dynasties, "the governments were weak, instead of strong, as far as their efforts in the increase of the financial income is concerned." Research Associate Cao Guilin of the Institute of History, CASS, said that Wang's paper had several debatable points. For example, Wang had divided the population of feudal society into two social strata. There was "officialdom" on the one hand and the "populace" on the other, representing two classes. But such a differentiation, Cao said, was insufficient to encompass the entire social structure during the period in question. There were people who owned large quantities of land for the purpose of exploitation of the peasants but who were not officials. What class, Cao asked, did these people belong to? He also pointed out that Wang's conclusions, that "there were very few instances of rebellion resulting purely from the heavy tax (or grain tax) exerted on the peasants" and, secondly, that the difference between "the officialdom" and "the populace" lay in whether or not "they paid the grain tax," both needed "further consideration when we look at the realities of Chinese history."

There was general development of a feudal tenant-landlord relationship which began during the Song dynasty. What was such a development like? In an effort to answer this question, Professor Qi Xia of the Department of History, Hebei University, presented a paper entitled "The Form of Land Rent and Its Evolution During the Song Dynasty." Professor Qi held that production relations during the Song differed because of the unbalanced development of labor productivity between various regions. Production was still backward in the southwest such as in Kuizhou *lu*[1] in Sichuan, where serfdom was still widely practiced and labor tax occupied a big percentage of all taxes. In most of the eastern region, a tenant-landlord system was well established in which tax in the form of an agreed percentage on output was prevalent. In the Eastern Zhejiang *lu* and Western Zhejiang *lu*, fixed taxes in the form of money came into existence. But generally speaking, rent paid in kind still occupied the dominant position during the Song dynasty and so did the natural economy. The emergence of rent in money reflected a noticeable development of a commodity economy when compared to previous dynasties, but it still played a minor role in the entire economy. As production developed, however, new economic relations, i.e., the buddings of capitalism, could come into existence in the most developed regions. But owing to the high rate of feudal exploitation and the low level of labor productivity, the individual producer encountered great difficulties in his effort to increase production. Therefore, Professor Qi concluded that the fundamental reason why China had remained a feudal society for such a long time was the stagnate role played by the feudal system of economic exploitation.

Professor Robert Hartwell of the University of Pennsylvania commented positively on Qi's paper, saying that the author had studied tablet inscriptions which had been rarely touched upon by others and that the author had corrected the ideas of some Japanese historians in this field. As further proof of Qi's conclusions, Ran Guangrong of the History Department, Sichuan University, presented to the symposium the results of his own investigation into certain national minority districts in Sichuan. Professor Deng Guangming, however, did not agree with Qi's conclusion. He argued that Qi's example—money rents paid to schools in lieu of grain in Wuzhou—is an exceptional situation, not typical of the relationship between landlords and tenants. It deserves further exploration.

Two papers were presented at the symposium dealing with the tenant-landlord relationship during the Ming and Qing dynasties which used contract documents of land sales as a basis for research. One was entitled "A

---

[1] *Lu* was an administrative region immediately under Song imperial government.

Preliminary Analysis of Tenant-Landlord Relationships in Ming and Qing China," written by Fu-mei Chang Chen, Research Associate of the Hoover Institution, Stanford University. The other was entitled "A Preliminary Study of the Unofficial Land Sales in Northern Fujian During the Qing Dynasty," written by Lecturer Yang Guozhen of the Department of History, Shamen (Amoy) University. Basing their studies on unofficial contracts of land sales, the two authors arrived at totally different conclusions. Fu-mei Chang Chen wrote that "these contracts strongly suggest that both parties gained greatly by their agreeing to certain property rights to the land and fulfulling obligations to each other," that "it is extremely difficult to argue on the basis of the evidence presented so far in the literature that long-term trends of landlord exploitation of tenants had existed during either the Ming or Qing periods," and that "as long as the tenants remained free to choose amongst their alternatives before entering into a contract, I believe we are not justified in calling them the 'exploited class.' " Yang Guozhen disagreed with such conclusions, saying that tenant-landlord relationships formed under different conditions could be totally different and that the analysis of permanent tenancy could hardly cover all the economic relations between landlords and tenants. During the short period when rents were not fixed, Yang said, tenants were left in a position of insecurity and faced ruin at any time. Moreover, in judging the relations between the two contractual parties, we should not only look at the words written into the contracts, but also consider the many possible ways in which landlords could exert pressure on tenants according to unwritten and customary laws. Privileged landlords with social status had much stronger control over tenants than ordinary landlords. Research Associate Liu Yongcheng and others agreed with Professor Chang that it was inappropriate to describe all tenants during the Ming and Qing dynasties as serfs. On the other hand, they cited many examples to prove that peasants under a shared-rent system were in fact reduced to serfdom.

Notwithstanding the fact that peasants bound by a tenant relationship were not entirely equivalent to agricultural serfs, Lecturer Ye Xian'en of the Department of History, Zhongshan University, contended that there were serfs in the true sense during the Ming and Qing dynasties or towards the end of the period of Chinese feudal society. In "A Report on the Investigation of the Tenant System in Chawan Village, Qimen County, and Mingzhou Village, Xiuning County, of Huizhou," Ye gave a detailed and interesting introduction to his investigations of these two places.[2] Xie Guozhen, Research Fellow at the Institute of History, made a supplementary speech on this subject based on documents from the late Ming dynasty.

---

[2] The report was published in the Chinese edition of *Social Sciences in China*, no. 1 (1981), with the title "The Tenant-Servant System in Huizhou Prefecture," and its English version will be in our journal, no. 1 (1981).

Kinship was another important topic concerning rural society which was discussed at the symposium. One paper on this subject, "Social Structure, Kinship, and Local-Level Politics in Ming-Qing," was presented by Jerry Dennerline, Assistant Professor of History at Pomona College. Chinese participants were interested to learn about the study of the Chinese kinship system by American scholars, especially the methodology Dennerline used in his research and analysis of the lineage and community changes of the Hua family in Wuxi county over several hundred years. But Dennerline's article also provoked two questions for debate. First, some Chinese scholars were of the opinion that, although there was a weakening of the kinship system during the Ming and Qing, as Dennerline had concluded in his paper, there was also a strengthening of the rural kinship system in certain districts beginning in the Song dynasty. Wang Sizhi, Associate Professor at the Institute of Qing History of the Chinese People's University, pointed out that this was the result of conscious encouragement by the ruling class and government support; "with the daily sharpening contradictions between tenants and landlords," the rural kinship system "developed primarily as a result of landlord efforts to control the peasants." As to the nature of the kinship system, Dennerline emphasized "the respect for the clan and protection of the lineage" and economic cooperation within the clan. Some Chinese scholars, however, argued that the political function of the kinship system should also be emphasized. Research Fellow Li Wenzhi of the Institute of Economics, CASS, said that feudal governments endowed the head of a clan with the power to settle local disputes and certain powers to judge criminal cases. Kinship was usually combined with the *baojia* system (an administrative system organized on the basis of households, with each *jia* made up of ten households and each *bao* of ten *jia*) and the landlords' militia for the purpose of safeguarding the rule of the landlord class and preventing peasant insurrections. The kinship system therefore had the characteristics of a political organization at the grassroots level and became a tool in the hands of the landlord class to rule over the peasants.

2. Problems Concerning the Cities, the Monetary System, Price Levels, and Foreign Trade

Three articles were on cities of the Song dynasty, of which two dealt with the city of Kaifeng, capital of the Northern Song. One was entitled "Kaifeng Around the Eleventh Century," written by Research Associate Chen Zhen of the Institute of History of Henan province. The other was entitled "The Economic Development of the Eastern Capital of the Song Dynasty and Its Role in Economic and Cultural Exchanges with Foreign Countries," by Lecturer Zhou Baozhu of the Department of History, Henan Teachers' University. As time was limited, only the first paper was read and discussed. With the help of many historical records listed in *Song huiyao jigao* [The draft collection of rules and regulations of the Song dynasty] and other sources, Chen Zhen analyzed the city of Kaifeng circa the eleventh century in respect to population size, the scale, structure, and internal relations of production of handicraft workshops, and the city system. Chen said that Kaifeng during the eleventh century "was a typical city of the late Middle Ages, which in certain respects already possessed some elements of the new capitalist relations of production." As commentator on this paper, Professor Skinner thought differently. He said that "it [Kaifeng] could hardly be considered a typical city. Rather, it was quite a specific case." Skinner talked about the methodology that should be used in the study of cities like Kaifeng, saying that in an analysis of productive forces and the relations of production in these cities, one "should take the whole surrounding region as a unit, because the relations of production in the city and its hinterland developed side by side." Research Assistant Wang Zengyu of the Institute of History raised with Chen Zhen the problem of divided rule over the cities and the countryside and the problem of *xiangguan* or *xiangli* (officials at the grassroots level in the cities). Professor Cheng Yingliu of the Department of History, Shanghai Teachers' College, in his paper "Two Examples of the Development of Cities in the Song Dynasty" made an in-depth analysis of the *jiandang guan* (superintendent in a village or town not up to the full status of an official) and *xiangguan* of the Song dynasty, which helped explain from one aspect the development of Song cities.

It is commonly accepted that *jiaozi*, which appeared during the Northern Song period, was the earliest form of paper money in the world. Although much has been written on this subject, many puzzles remain. One of these is the circulation period of *jiaozi*. In trying to find an answer to this question, Research Associate Wang Zengyu argued in his paper, "Some Problems Concerning *Jiaozi* in the Northern Song Period," that "during the stage of its private administration, the time span for the circulation was about three years. Beginning from the first year of Tiansheng (1023) when *jiaozi* was administered by the government, the time span became two years. . . . Such a time span of two years continued into the Southern Song period." Professor Hartwell was greatly interested in Wang's paper and made some important contributions. Hartwell said that his own research demonstrated that the emergence of paper money enriched Chinese monetary theory, which in turn had a decisive impact on European monetary theory.

The circulation of silver as the major form of currency during the Ming dynasty is an important topic for research into the social and economic history of this period. In his paper "Time and Money: Another Approach to the Periodization of Ming History," William S. Atwell, Lecturer in the School of Oriental and African Studies of London University, analyzed the problem from two aspects: first, the influence of domestic mining and imported bullion on the monetary system of the Ming dynasty, and second, the division of the Ming dynasty into eight historical periods based on the circulation of silver. The commentator held that Atwell basically was outlining economic development in general and the financial evolution of the Ming government on the basis of such valuable statistical materials as tax income on silver, silver deposited in the state treasury, the output of silver mining, and the influx of silver from foreign countries. But most of the Chinese scholars had reservations about his method of using silver to judge the booms and slacks in the economy in order to periodize Ming history. Li Xun, Associate Professor of Jilin Teachers' University, said that periodization of the Ming dynasty is an extremely sophisticated matter and that silver circulation is only one of the many factors which must be considered. Mr. Atwell's periodization, he said, could only be considered as a periodization of the history of silver rather than that of the Ming economy. He also pointed out that the credibility of official figures on the circulation and import of silver should not be overstressed, although they did reflect some changes in the economy. Research Associate Liu Chongri of the Institute of History made the following two points concerning silver circulation. First, the value of silver as money and as means of circulation constantly fluctuated because of changes in supply and demand. For example, in the early years of the reign of Chongzhen (1628-1644), one *dou* (decaliter) of rice was worth a thousand *qian* (copper coins). Later the price went up to two thousand until it finally reached sixteen thousand. During the reign of Zhengtong (1436-1449), one tael of silver could buy three *dan* (hectoliter) of rice. But during the reign of Wanli (1573-1620), one tael of silver was not enough to buy one *dan* of rice. Under such circumstances, the amount of money used meant no more than the fact that prices had gone up. Second, in the Ming dynasty when the natural economy predominated, landlords tended to hoard money as a means of accumulating wealth rather than investing in material production. The output of silver mining and the influx of silver from foreign countries could hardly be used as economic barometers.

Professor Yeh-chien Wang of the Department of History, Kent State University, has carried out specialized research on grain prices. With the help of modern computer technology and three assistants, he has worked for three years to write his paper on "The Secular Movement of Grain Prices in China, ca. 1760-1910," using three hundred thousand pieces of information on grain prices as his data base. Beginning with an analysis of the Qing-dynasty grain price reporting system, Professor Wang made an in-depth analysis of grain price movement over a 150-year period from 1760 to 1910, working out the grain price indexes for several prefectures in the southeastern part of the country. He proceeded to analyze the variables that affected grain prices, such as population changes, money supply, grain output in different regions, trade, and the various policies adopted by the government to stabilize grain prices.

Participants at the symposium agreed that Professor Wang's work was of high academic value and hoped that he could go further with his research. Research Fellow Peng Zeyi of the Institute of Economics of the CASS made a six-point commentary on Wang's paper. He said that in an analysis of the secular movement of grain prices based on statistics, one should also take into consideration the fact that such statistics might embody much more sophisticated social and economic content and class relations. Sayings like "cheap grain harms the peasant" and "expensive grain starves the peasant," Peng said, are vivid evidence that the rise and fall of grain prices had an important bearing on agricultural production and the livelihood of the peasants. Ju Deyuan of the Chinese History Archives and Fan Shuzhi, Lecturer of the Department of History, Fudan University, also commented on Wang's paper.

Although many papers presented at the symposium touched on the question of China's foreign trade, only one paper dealt explicitly with this subject. Professor Yan Zhongping presented a paper entitled "The Opium War and China's Trade with the Western Countries, 1840-1860," in which he argued that there were no legitimate trade relations between China and the Western countries during this period. The bloody and illegal trade of this period was backed by gunships and protected by consulate jurisdiction and the consulate customs system (tax payable through the consulate). Basically it was primitive plunder of semicolonist China by Western countries. The majority of the merchants who came to China were adventurers sent by industrial and commercial capitalists in their home countries. Most of these merchants were scoundrels, ruffians, hooligans, gangsters, pirates, drunkards, and criminals who were engaged in armed smuggling, blackmail, extortion, robbery, kidnapping, rape, and murder. In a word, these people were the dregs of humanity who tried to create, under the protection of their national flags and gunships, an "adventurers' paradise" where they could freely smuggle opium, sell human beings, evade taxes, and engage in cold-blooded murder and all manner of evils. This so-called "free trade" was, in essence, the freedom to plunder. Professor Yan challenged the idea held by some historians that it was the Opium War which opened the door of China to Western merchants who conquered the handicraft industry by bringing inexpensive and high-quality industrial products to the Chinese market. Such a viewpoint, Professor Yan pointed out, inflates the progressive nature of Western technology and neglects the tenacity of China's original economic structure. In order to avoid nationalistic bias and one-sidedness in the choice of materials, Yan based his research entirely on materials available in foreign languages.

As commentator on Yan's paper, Professor Feuerwerker agreed with his denunciation of aggression by Western powers. Feuerwerker said:

> He correctly pointed out the plunderous nature of the trade between China and the Western countries between 1840 and 1860. . . . He is

absolutely justified to morally lash out against the opium and slave trade, smuggling, and the discrimination by foreign consulates and merchants against Chinese officials and people. . . . Even judging from the prevailing values of that period, the adventurers who opened the door of China could not be considered honorable gentlemen.

Feuerwerker, however, differed with Yan on the consequences of the trade between China and the Western countries. Feuerwerker argued that during the years between 1840 and 1860, foreigners did not conquer the Chinese market. It was only in later years that China became a major market for foreign countries and this was realized through legitimate trade. Most probably, foreign merchants did not make as great a profit as their Chinese counterparts in this legitimate trade. As a matter of fact, local commercial networks were developed instead of damaged, because most of the foreign merchants at the trading ports became agents of the service network of rich Chinese merchants in Shanghai and Hong Kong. Private investment from foreign countries beginning in the late nineteenth century may also have benefited China's economy. Pure trade, Feuerwerker went on, if we look at it as a whole, was beneficial to both parties concerned. International trade, foreign investment in manufacturing industries and transportation, and the introduction of new technology were beneficial to China and would have greatly promoted China's production if there had been an efficient central government. Feuerwerker concluded that "foreign economic power was only one of the factors that made China weak and corrupt, and not the major factor."

Professor Yan Zhongping and many Chinese scholars had considerable reservations about Professor Feuerwerker's comments. But because Feuerwerker's remarks came at the end of the six-day symposium, time did not permit further discussion.

3. Relations Between the Feudal State and the Economy

Relations between the feudal state and the economy was another important subject discussed at the symposium. Of the six papers presented on this topic, five were limited to a period covered by only one regime. An overall analysis of the entire period was made by Professor Feuerwerker in the sixth paper, "The State and the Economy in Late Imperial China," which sparked a heated discussion. In his paper, Feuerwerker placed the nearly one thousand years since the Song dynasty within the scope of world history, examining relations between governments of various dynasties and their economies. He arrived at four conclusions. First, China's premodern economic growth from the Song onward was remarkable, although uneven in both rate and locale. Second, the policies and actions of the imperial government were not unreasonable when compared to the early modern European experience, insofar as they concern premodern economic development. On balance, they probably helped rather than hindered the long-term growth of population and total output. Third, neither the direct nor indirect influences of the state on the economy were the major factors determining the nature and rate of growth. This was largely decided by the dynamics of the dominant private sector of the economy. And fourth, the state contributed little if anything towards modern economic growth in contrast to the history of early modern Europe, but its failings were probably less exploitation and oppression than omission and incompetence.

The Chinese scholars were greatly interested in the research method used by Professor Feuerwerker. Professor Deng Guangming said that Feuerwerker's paper, as well as many others written by his American colleagues, "are unlike the articles or books written by Chinese historians in both the selection of research topics and the breadth and depth of time and space covered. Chinese historians tend to be rigid, reserved, and constrained in their writing." Reading the kind of articles written by Feuerwerker can widen our perspective, Deng said, although many participants found it difficult to agree with Feuerwerker's conclusions. Professor Deng argued that Feuerwerker had underestimated government control and influence over the economy since the Northern Song period and overestimated the role of the commodity economy. Citing some examples, Deng pointed out that "the leading element in the social economy of the Song dynasty was agriculture and not commodity economy. Government influence on agriculture was far from 'limited.' " As revealed by voluminous household registration records among the recently discovered documents from Dunhuang of Gansu province and Turpan of Xinjiang Autonomous Region, Deng said, it was incorrect to say that the state had only "direct control over the population in the big cities, and the population in the countryside was beyond their reach."

Research Associate Li Jiaju of the Institute of History backed up Professor Deng's argument with a lot of historical data, stressing the negative role played by Song governments in the development of commodity economy:

> The embargo on the Liao during the Northern Song and on the Jin during the Southern Song periods, regardless of the existence of a smuggling trade, did have a detrimental effect on the circulation of commodities. Take commercial taxes for example. During the reign of Xining (1068-1077), there were over 2,000 tax organizations in counties, prefectures, towns, and cities, not counting "tax shops" (*shuipu*) or "tax places" (*shuichang*) at ordinary market fairs. Southern Song merchants described tax places as "execution sites," indicating that there was an extremely heavy suppression of commerce and commodity economy at the time.

Associate Professor Wei Qingyuan of Chinese People's University was of the opinion that in researching such a problem, one should deal with the positive as well as the negative role of governments in economic development, saying that "an over- or under-estimation of either would be wrong. The important thing is to make a concrete analysis." Sociology Professor Gilbert Rozman of Princeton University did not agree with Professor Feuerwerker's estimation that the development of Chinese cities during the Ming and Qing dynasties was similar to that of premodern cities in Europe. He said that the Qing dynasty had not reached its peak of development as a premodern society. Feuerwerker's comparison of the influence of the Qing state over the social economy and seventeenth-century Europe and Japan hardly supports his conclusions. "Such a comparison is not convincing," Rozman said. Professor Yeh-chien Wang agreed with Rozman and said that Ming and Qing governments aimed not at the promotion of production, but at stabilizing their rule through ethical principles.

Among the papers which dealt with the influence of certain state policies of a given dynasty on the social economy, Professor Deng Guangming's was unique in that it analyzed the influence of the military system on the social economy. In his paper "The Relationship of the Mercenary System of the Northern Song Period to Social Weaknesses, Poverty, and Agricultural Production," Deng concluded that the existence of a standing army of 1.4 million was one of the causes of social weaknesses because in the Northern Song period a policy of mutual constraint was practiced between top government officials and the generals and commanders of the Imperial Army, between troops garrisoned in the capital and those in other parts of the country, between the commanders and the soldiers, and between the commanders of the three military forces and the officials in charge of national defense.

Another important factor was the change in conscription policy. Before this period, soldiers were conscripted from the peasantry for definite terms of duty. In the Northern Song a new policy to develop a professional army was adopted. As a result, over a million so-called "able-bodied men" were drafted, and there was a serious lack of hands for agricultural production throughout the country and "large quantities of fertile land lay wasted" in the central part of the country. This was one of the causes of the impoverishment of the dynasty.

Professor Brian McKnight of Hawaii University pointed out that historians had seldom linked research on the military system with economic problems and that Professor Deng had taken an important step by doing so for the first time. Adding to Deng's analysis, McKnight said that since Kaifeng as a capital was strategically vulnerable, a large army had to be garrisoned there for its defense, resulting in large expenditures for the maintenance of a gigantic army and bringing social economic development to a halt. McKnight asked Deng and all other historians who claimed that the Song dynasty was weak: "Was the Song dynasty really weak?" Looking back at all the feudal dynasties in Chinese history, he said, one discovers that the Song was the only dynasty which was not threatened by insurrections and uprisings from within. This demonstrated that the Song was not weak. The fact that the Song government failed to drive out the Liao invaders, lost its northern territory to the Jin, and later surrendered to the Mongolians was not proof that it was really weak, because weakness is only a relative term for a state under armed aggression from without. The Liao and Jin were among the most powerful states in the world at the time. The Mongolians had the finest military machine in history. Professor McKnight argued that the very fact that the Song resisted the invincible Mongolian armies on the battlefield for as long as thirty years and, moreover, was not finally defeated by a frontal attack across its main defenses but by a flank encirclement in the western part of the country, demonstrated that the Song dynasty was not really weak, "it was only not very strong."

Three other papers analyzed the socioeconomic impact of specific policies adopted by the ruling classes: "The System of Tax on Grain Transported from South China via the Grand Canal During the Ming Dynasty," by Bao Yanbang of the Department of History, Jinan University; "Wasteland Reclamation Policies and Achievements During the Reigns of Shunzhi (1644-1661) and Kangxi (1662-1722)," by Guo Songyi, Research Assistant at the Institute of History; and "The Rise and Development of the 'Single-Whip' Tax Reform (yitiaobian fa)," by Fan Shuzhi of the Department of History, Fudan University. Bao Yanbang held that the system of tax on grain transported via the Grand Canal in the Ming dynasty was in essence the feudal rulers' brutal exploitation of the peasants by tax and corvée. His article described the heavy burden of grain taxes on provinces where there was a water transportation system and the major influences of such a system on the agrarian economy and class struggle in these areas. Under the double burden of both the heavy tax in kind and the "levy for what was not produced," the peasants were forced to exhaust their energies and resources on household handicraft industry involving also the growing of cotton and the weaving of cloth. As a result, they were drawn into the developing commodity economy and markets and became subject to the heavy exploitation of commercial capital and the usurers, and their own development was curbed. Guo Songyi pointed out that when great numbers of peasants became destitute and homeless, large pieces of land lay idle and production was seriously damaged, as in the last years of the Ming dynasty. The policy of wasteland reclamation adopted by the Qing government in its early years helped the rapid recovery and development of the social economy so that a new height of economic development was realized in the later years of Emperor Kangxi. Beginning from the latter half of the seventeenth century to the end of the eighteenth century, the Qing government was economically strong and able to put down rebellions at home and resist aggression from abroad. Under the unified Qing state there was political stability and economic development, known in Chinese history as "the times of peace and prosperity under the reign of Qianlong" (1736-1795). Quoting from many local historical sources, Mr. Fan concluded in his study of the rise and development of the "single-whip" tax reform that it was a product of the advancement of commodity and monetary economy before the mid-Ming dynasty and that the realization of such a reform in turn "promoted further development of the commodity and monetary economy, expediting the process of commercialization of agricultural products and the expansion of commodity markets."

Discussion of governments and their policies inevitably led to an analysis of the ruling classes. In this respect, Professor Brian McKnight made an indepth analysis in his article "Song Legal Privileges" of such privileges as Deliberation *(yi)*, Petition *(qing)*, Reduction *(jian)*, and Commutation *(shu)* enjoyed by the "ruling elite" (i.e., officials and their families) of the Song dynasty when they committed crimes. He described the distribution and changes of these privileges. Wang Zengyu, Zhou Baozhu, and Research Associate Jing Junjian of the Institute of Economics, CASS, showed great interest in McKnight's article and made some comments and suggestions.

4. Problems of Population and Literacy

Two papers on population problems in Chinese history were presented to the symposium. One was by Professor Robert Hartwell, entitled "Patterns of Settlement, the Structure of Government, and the Social Transformation of the Chinese Political Elite, ca. 750-1550." The other was Gilbert Rozman's "Historical Demography: Sources and Indicators for the Study of the Qing Population." Hartwell emphasized in his article that, like the changes in the political, economic, and social systems, the demographic changes which were closely related to the economic development of a society also followed discernible laws. Similarly, changes in the distribution of the population invariably brought about changes in the political structure and the structure of officialdom. Hartwell gave an overview of the changes and movements of the population over seven-hundred-odd years, trying to find out how shifts in demographic distribution, development of the economy, and changes in the political structure "gave rise to a transformation in the composition and behavior of the political elite." As commentators on Hartwell's paper, Professor Cheng Yingliu and Cong Hanxiang, Research Assistant of the Institute of Modern History, CASS, agreed with Hartwell that there are discernible laws which govern the development of history. They said that unless such laws are discovered, there can be no real understanding of history. These Chinese historians, however, differed with Hartwell on the following questions: power transfer from the central government to local governments since the Song dynasty; the existence of professional bureaucrats during this period; the reasons behind the innovations of science and technology during the Song dynasty and their stagnation during ensuing decades; the reasons why economic development during the Song dynasty did not lead to a fundamental change in the social structure; the question of whether during the Ming there was a shift of population from the Huanghe River (Yellow River) valley to the lower reaches of the Changjiang River (Yangzi River); and the question of whether there existed a linear relationship between the growth of population and the formation of villages and hamlets in terms of demographic statistics.

Many Chinese historians were greatly interested in Rozman's introduction to the results and present status of research on historical demography by Western historians since the 1950s. But most of the Chinese historians disagreed with one of Rozman's main points:

> Under the impetus of contributions in each of these areas, it is now taken for granted that conclusions about many of the central problems of social history need to be restated not only in per capita terms but also in terms of their relationship to conditions resulting in population growth or decline. Social scientists are rewriting diverse areas of history, e.g., economic history, urban history, social class history, and family history, in the light of demographic findings.

Talking about rewriting Chinese history with full consideration of population variables, he wrote, "It would, perhaps, not be much of an exaggeration to claim that in certain circles the expectations that once focused on reinterpreting China's past in terms of class conflict are now centered on population and related variables." Professor Chen Zhenhan of the Department of Economics, Beijing University, countered that quantitative or qualitative changes in population could not possibly be the decisive factor for the advancement of history. Neither could it lead to a redetermination of the outline of Chinese economic history. Although population is an important element of the productive forces in terms of economic development, it cannot be considered an immutable or simple, one-sided determinant. Professor Chen asked, "If different paths and rates of economic development can be explained merely in terms of population, why was it that China and Japan, both densely populated, achieved totally different results from their economic reforms carried out in the late nineteenth century? Why was it that there were constant social revolutions in China in the twentieth century whereas Japan basically stuck to the prevailing social and economic system?" Professor Chen claimed that history should be interpreted in two ways, one way in terms of final causality and the other relative causality. The theory of class struggle deals with final causality and emphasizes that the motivating force of social development is the contradiction between productive forces and the relations of production. Within this general framework, one can discover many relative causalities. Professor Peng Zeyi said:

> Within a certain period of time, the natural growth rate of the population increases as a result of socioeconomic development. Disproportion between growth rates of population and social productivity would impede

the development of the social economy. The problem of population and its growth certainly influenced Chinese history, but such influence was not decisive and cannot be used in lieu of "class conflicts" in the study and interpretation of history.

Professors Chen and Peng as well as Ju Deyuan also raised some questions about the Qing population data used by Rozman and his evaluation of these materials.

"Education, Functional Literacy, and Their Economic and Social Effects," by Evelyn S. Rawski of Pittsburgh University, was the only paper presented at the symposium dealing with relations between education and the social economy. Giving an overall treatment of the problem of popularization of literacy beginning from the year 202 B.C. until the Ming and Qing dynasties, Rawski maintained that education and functional literacy were promoted along with the development of the social economy. Highly developed printing technology and publishing facilities gave a noticeable push towards the popularization of functional literacy. Rawski also discussed in her article the relationship between functional literacy and modernization. Associate Professor Hong Huanchun of the Department of History, Nanjing University, disagreed with Rawski's conclusion that the imperial examination system, the bureaucratic system, and the *baojia* system played key roles in the popularization of literacy. He said that these systems were negative factors which impeded the popularization of functional literacy. Hong suggested that different situations in the various historical periods should be treated differently in studying the effects of popularization of literacy on the social economy. Hong raised another question for discussion: Why was it that Ming and Qing China was still far from becoming an industrialized society despite the fact that since ancient times China had a relatively advanced cultural and educational level which had produced great educators like Confucius? Wang Rongsheng, Research Associate at the Institute of History, said that beginning from the Song dynasty, the publication of great numbers of primers did help raise literacy and educational levels, but the socioeconomic impact of education and the popularization of literacy should be analyzed in terms of the content and methods prevailing in education at that time. The purpose of education was to enable people to read and become government officials. The main content was ethical education rather than the teaching of practical knowledge. The method was mechanical memorizing. As a result, many people could recite passages from books but could not read much. Under such circumstances, education and functional literacy did not strongly influence social production and the social economy.

Adding to Wang's comments, Professor Yang Xiangkui, a specialist in Chinese intellectual history and the history of Chinese education, said that ancient Chinese education can be divided into two categories—education in morals and values and education in crafts and skills. Many Confucian educationists since the Han dynasty were well-known scientists who contributed a great deal to the development of ancient science and technology. But such a development came to a stop after the Tang dynasty. China led the world in science and technology until the Song dynasty, when education in crafts and skills gave way to that in morals and values and education started to go downhill. Things went from bad to worse during the Qing, when science and technology were considered as "fantasies and dirty tricks," thus widening the gap to world scientific and technological levels. Many of the participants were convinced by Professor Yang's analysis. Others maintained that China's science and technology did not become backward until after the Song dynasty because there were three great inventions during the Song dynasty. Professor Feuerwerker said, however, that the concentration on education in morals and values hardly explains why China's science and technology declined from originally advanced levels. He argued that the church in medieval Europe likewise promoted only education in morals and values and not education in crafts and skills.

5. The Development of Commodity Economy
and the Sprouts of Capitalism

A central topic for discussion at the symposium was the sprouts of capitalism in China. Nine papers were presented on this subject.

In his article "China's Landlord Economy and the Sprouts of Agrarian Capitalism,"[3] Li Wenzhi, Research Fellow at the Institute of Economics, CASS, based his analysis on the transition from feudal employment to free employment. He discussed the emergence of the sprouts of capitalism in agriculture during the Ming and Qing dynasties with reference to the characteristics of Chinese feudal society in general and feudal landownership in particular. He said that during Ming and Qing times, feudal land relations as reflected in feudal lineage, tenant-landlord, and feudal dependent relations between employers and employees were shaken up. Three groups of people were engaged in agricultural management at that time: rich peasants, common landlords, and landlordlected in feudal lineage, tenant-landlord, and feudal dependent relations between employers and employees were shaken up. Three groups of people were engaged in agricultural management at that time: rich peasants, common landlords, and landlord officials. During the mid-Ming, the practice of free employment instead of feudal employment first appeared among rich

---

[3] The article was published in the Chinese edition of *Social Sciences in China*, no. 1 (1981), and its English version will appear in our journal, no. 1 (1981).

peasants. In the early years of the Qing dynasty, when common landlordism flourished, free employment relations also materialized. The advance from rich peasants to common landlords in the management of agriculture was a clear manifestation of development of the sprouts of China's agrarian capitalism. The reasons for the slowness of the advance and the ultimate stagnation of the process, Li said, were the fetters of the landlord economy and oppressive control by the machinery of the centralized state.

Professor Feuerwerker said that while giving a detailed treatment of the changes in the relations of production, Li failed to provide a detailed treatment of the actual state of productive forces and technical possibilities. According to Feuerwerker, one of the reasons why China's agriculture did not become capitalist was that China did not experience an "agrarian revolution" like Europe did before it entered its modern period. In the study of this problem, a distinction must be made between the increase of crop yield per unit area and the increase of the average crop yield per laborer. A real agrarian revolution happens only when there is a big increase in average yield per laborer. Feuerwerker concluded:

> The possibility for an agrarian revolution was obstructed by the disadvantageous ratio of population to land. . . . Even without such negative factors as the lineage system and the imperial government, certain conditions related to the productive forces themselves could have resulted in the stagnation of China's agriculture from Ming-Qing to the twentieth century.

If Li's article did in fact fail to give adequate treatment to the productive forces, the four articles presented by Peng Zeyi, Li Xun, Hong Huanchun, and Cong Hanxiang made up for it by combining research on the relations and forces of production.

In his article "The Development of Industry and Commerce and the Sprouts of Capitalism in Suzhou During the Ming and Qing Dynasties," Hong Huanchun, on the basis of tablet inscriptions preserved in Suzhou prefecture, studied the development of the handicraft industry and commerce and the sprouts of capitalism. He pointed out that the emergence of many *huiguan* and *gongsuo* (guild halls for craftsmen and merchants) after the reign of Wanli (1573-1620) was an inevitable result of commodity competition. These guilds served to propel the development of industry and commerce, and during the late Qing and early Republican periods, these further developed to become capitalist chambers of commerce. Discussants agreed that the methodology used by Mr. Hong in digging deep into a case study was highly commendable.

In his article "The Development of the Handicraft Industry in the First Half of the Qing Dynasty," Professor Peng Zeyi made a quantitative as well as qualitative study of the restoration and development of handicraft industry and mining and the changes in the relations of production during the Qing. He divided the first half of the Qing dynasty into four economic periods. Peng explained how a portion of the commercial capital was transferred from circulation into production, so that policies undertaken during the first half of the Qing dynasty towards the handicraft industries were favorable to the promotion of production. A big step forward was the emergence in the 1820s and 1830s of a series of industrial and mineral enterprises with budding relations of capitalist production. But because the feudal and self-sufficient natural economy still prevailed during the Qing, these budding relations of capitalist production were still not strong enough to shake and dissolve the existing social and economic system. Professor Skinner commented that it was evident from Peng's paper that, beginning with the Tang and Song dynasties, the involvement of officials in production steadily declined so that the general trend was the gradual withdrawal of government from direct engagement in economic management, a trend seen not only in commerce, but also in handicraft industries. What was unique about the Qing dynasty in contrast to earlier dynasties was the fact that from the very beginning the government took a laissez-faire stand with respect to economic management and did not change this policy even after recovery of the economy. Such a laissez-faire stand permitted a much more reduced involvement on the part of government in economic administration compared with previous dynasties. Professor Skinner argued that this was a conscious, far-sighted, and significant policy and concluded, therefore, that "the Manchus promoted instead of stopping the economic development of China." He said that Peng's article lacked "a clarification of the structures of the economy in various localities during the different periods."

In her article "A Preliminary Study of the Development of the Cotton Planting and Textile Industries During the Ming Dynasty," Cong Hanxiang of the Institute of Modern History, CASS, explored how the cotton planting and textile industries became popularized during the Ming, asking why a breakthrough in the textile industry, which in Europe had led to an industrial revolution, was not possible in China. She wrote:

> During the Ming, cotton weaving was still in the form of household sideline production. Small-scale handicraftsmen specializing in cotton weaving did appear at the time, but their number was quite small; not only were handicraft factories nonexistent, we haven't even discovered the existence of small handicraft workshops with only one or two wage workers. The widespread existence of household cotton weaving as a kind of sideline occupation for peasants formed an important integral part of the small-scale peasant economy. . . . Any form of handicraft factory was doomed in competition with such sideline production which was closely integrated with agriculture and not limited by cost factors other than raw materials and simple tools.

Cong added that this resilience was further demonstrated by the resistance of China's cotton textile industry to the influx of advanced foreign textile goods after the Opium War.

Cong's paper was well received at the symposium and sparked heated discussion. Professor Yeh-chien Wang commented that, in the study of the competition between China's cotton textile industry and foreign cotton goods after the Opium War, "the backwardness of China's transportation also played a protective role," apart from the household sideline features of the industry. He challenged Cong's conclusion that "small workshops having only one or two employed textile workers were nonexistent," saying that this was contrary to historical fact. Associate Professor Philip Huang of the University of California said that commercialization of agriculture can lead to class polarization. He argued that on the one hand, cotton planting was much more profitable than grain planting, making it possible for some of the small owner-peasants to become middle or rich peasants or even manager landlords; on the other hand, the cost of cotton planting was much higher than that of grain planting, making it more risky to engage in cotton planting, and some of the owner-peasants could become poor peasants or tenants as a result of natural or man-made calamities. Poverty would lead to further commercialization, because a poor peasant in order to subsist would have to grow a higher percentage of cash crops. Huang raised another question: How can we explain why in China, unlike Western Europe, industry did not emerge in areas where a premodern (handicraft) industry was highly developed?

The Ming and Qing dynasties witnessed major changes in the social economy, which in turn produced new social groupings that deserve special study. Four papers were presented at the symposium on these social groups. Associate Professor Li Xun of Jilin Teachers' University maintained in his "On the Forces of the Jiangnan (South of the Changjiang River) Group" that the unprecedented development of an urban monetary economy in the area south of the Changjiang River during the Ming dynasty caused two kinds of divisions: manager landlords and rich peasants, who split off from the landlord class, and townspeople of different strata, such as the employed handicraft workers, workshop owners, commercial capitalists, etc., who split off from small-scale producers. In their struggle against the aristocratic landlords, the landlord gentry, manager landlords, and big merchants, handicraft workshop owners and the masses of the employed handicraft workers gradually became a political force in the southern Changjiang River area. The formation of such a force was a reflection of the economic and political struggles of this historical period. This force met with constant setbacks which greatly affected not only the development of the economy in the Jiangnan area, but more important, the development of the entire Chinese society. Bao Yanbang felt that Li's article successfully reflected the complexity of the various classes and strata in the Jiangnan area, but he thought that Li could have treated in more detail the so-called manager landlords with respect to their emergence, methods of management, regional distribution, social characteristics, independence as an economic force, and their political viewpoints and demands. Dennerline pointed out that, although the aristocratic landlords, the landlord gentry, and the manager landlords all joined forces as mentioned in Li's paper, there were great differences among them in terms of political and economic demands. What, then, he asked, brought these three kinds of landlords together? What was their common interest? These were questions that deserved further discussion.

Lin Renchuan, Research Assistant at the Institute of History of Shamen University, challenged the orthodox view on wokou (Japanese pirates) in his paper "Private Sea Trade Merchants and the Wokou in the Ming Dynasty." He said that prior to the Jiajing period (1522-1566), wokou were simply Japanese pirates who harassed the Chinese coast. But the composition of wokou changed significantly after the Jiajing period as great numbers of bankrupt peasants and more and more private sea trade merchants turned to pirating. From then on, Japanese pirates constituted only 10 to 20 percent of the wokou. The rest were Chinese coastal residents whose activities were mainly in opposition to the embargo against coast trade and fishing. In essence, Lin said, the wokou wars during and after the Ming were struggles waged against the embargo and government oppression in general. As a result, governmental oppression and exploitation in the form of tax and corvée became, for the time being, less severe. Obstacles to the practice of the "single-whip" tax reform were removed. And the Ming government was forced to open up a few sea ports, thus promoting the development of private overseas trade and the commodity economy along the southeastern coastline.

Discussants pointed out that Lin's desire to challenge conventional understanding of the problem was commendable. Associate Professor Li Xun agreed that a considerable number of the wokou were peasants who were trying to make a living along the southeastern coast. But he said that the composition of wokou was quite complicated. Generally speaking, they consisted of three kinds of pirates: Chinese, Japanese, and pirates from the Western countries. A concrete analysis should be made, therefore, as to whether or not the nature of the struggles waged by the wokou was antiembargo. Mr. Atwell suggested that in the study of the Fujian coastal crisis, one must take the Sino-Japanese trade crisis into full consideration, because the two crises were inseparable. Bao Yanbang said, however, that the author had overestimated the struggle of the wokou and that the situation in the Jiajing period was quite different from that after Wanli's reign.

One of the important features of the paper by Wang Sizhi, Associate Professor at the Institute of Qing History, Chinese People's University, and Jin Chengji on "The Rise and Fall of the Salt Merchants Along the Huaihe River

During the First Half of the Qing Dynasty" was the choice of a social group which had great impact on the social economy of the Qing dynasty, exploring its rise and fall over a two-hundred-year period. They wrote that in the Qianlong period, because the policy of "protection of commerce in order to increase tax revenues" was seriously carried out, putting salt merchants under the protection of salt officials and the emperor, salt merchants along the Huaihe River developed into a commercial feudal monopoly with huge amounts of capital. The leading family of this commercial group became financial tycoons of the first half of the Qing dynasty. Beginning in the reign of Jiaqing (1769-1820), however, endless and ever-increasing taxes and levies as well as corruption and extortion on the part of officials brought about the final decline of the salt merchants along the Huaihe River. Mr. Rozman commented that the author failed to give adequate consideration to three variables (price, tax, and population) which are basic to research on economic history. He said that if the inflation rate, especially the rate of increase in grain prices, is not taken into account, it would be difficult to determine the actual rise of salt prices. Nor would it be possible to explain how the increase of salt prices was related to the increase of the population if we did not consider the question of population.

In "The Rise and Fall of Fan: The Noted Qing Imperial Merchant Family," Wei Qingyuan and Wu Qiyan conducted a case study of one of the richest and most influential merchant families of the early Qing dynasty. The authors' purpose was to study the laws of development of commercial capital and the reason why many rich Chinese merchants who had already been engaged in large-scale management in the eighteenth and nineteenth centuries failed to become modern capitalists and financial magnates. Fan was representative of big, backward merchants during the last years of feudal society in China. The decline of profits for such manager merchants was a sign that feudal classes in Chinese society were dying out. There was a distant sounding of the death knell for feudalism in China. Ye Xian'en and Jing Junjian commended the authors' use of unpublished archival materials to conduct a case study of the Fan clan in order to examine commercial capital, but thought that the authors had overestimated the percentage of commercial capital represented by such feudal merchants. Their conclusion, therefore, about the "narrow outlets" for Qing commercial capital is still open to question. William Atwell said that Wei and Wu's article not only gave an important introduction to early Qing economic history, but also suggested a possible solution to the controversy over government influence on the social economy. Judging from the various difficulties for the merchants created by senior government bureaucrats, it is clear, he concluded, that the government had a negative influence on the social economy.

6. Questions of Methodology in Doing Research
on Economic History

Among the many original and innovative articles presented at the symposium, "Marketing Systems and Regional Economics: Their Structure and Development" by Professor G. William Skinner of the Department of Anthropology, Stanford University, ranked first. Over the years, he has used a specific method in studying Chinese history—what he calls the regional systems approach. Such a method lays emphasis on functional analysis of the characteristics of economic regions themselves and their historical development in terms of a geographic/economic hierarchical scheme put forward by Skinner. He demonstrated that on the assumption of uniform demand density, market centers at any given level were spaced according to an isometric grid. Thus, the hinterlands tended to be hexagonal rather than circular in shape. A honeycomb of hexagonal hinterlands developed, each in contact with six others at the same level. Market centers at one level were interdependent upon neighbors at adjacent levels. Together these various levels of market grids formed what he called a macroregional system. The Chinese economic structure, when looked at from above, divided into eight levels, the lowest one being the standard market towns. The number of economic centers decreased sharply at each step up the hierarchy. The author divided nineteenth century China into nine macroregions: Lingnan, the Southeast Coast, the Lower Changjiang (Yangzi), the Middle Changjiang, the Upper Changjiang, Northwest, Southwest, North, and Northeast. Every macroregion had its "core" and "peripheries." Within the core area, there were more commercialized agricultural products and handicrafts on sale in markets. Skinner gave a detailed analysis of the Upper Changjiang macroregion centered around Chongqing, evaluating the size and arrangement of the marketing system and studying the empirewide structure of regional economies. He also analyzed the similarities and differences between the administrative hierarchy and the regional economic hierarchy. In order to safeguard their rule and prevent the expansion of local forces, the ruling circles intentionally divided the core of a macroregion into several parts, attaching them to different administrative provinces. This was the case in the Southeast Coast, which had been divided into the three provinces of Jiangsu, Zhejiang, and Anhui. In his analysis of Chinese history in terms of the development of macroregional systems, Skinner held that the cycles of development in different macroregions were seldom closely synchronized. He proposed, therefore, that the proper units for analysis in economic history were not prefectures or provinces, much less the empire as a whole. Adherence to administrative spatial demarcations and periodization by rule of dynasties was of no significance for the study of economic history. The rise and fall of dynasties, Skinner said, only affected some macroregions which followed similar cycles of development, but not all the macroregions. Apart from its own historical conditions, a macroregion's cycle of development was also affected by weather and natural calamities. Skinner summarized his understanding of China's regional economies in these terms: "Reality is almost infinitely differentiated, but that differentiation is not random."

Skinner's original methodology sparked great interest among participants. Professor Wang Yuquan said that this was a "scholastic writing rarely seen in history," one which adopts a macroregional system approach on the one hand and a microanalysis of Chinese history on the other. The most striking feature, Wang said, about this paper was the understanding of relations between parts, taking every part as a whole and pursuing the idea that certain laws can be discovered from the existence and movements of things. He did not agree, however, with Skinner's use of a single-model methodology, saying that "using only one model to embrace innumerable historical facts would tend to confine living history into a rigid framework, and once such a framework is formed, researchers might neglect those historical facts which go counter to the model, and research work might go astray from real historical developments." Moreover, Professor Wang stressed, commerce involved the process of commodity circulation and could not create any values. Its development was determined by the development of production. Therefore, using the market as a standard unit in various regions "can be applied to the Changjiang River basin but not to North China; it might be possible to apply it to modern China, but not to the Tang and Song dynasties." Professor Qi Xia maintained that the theory of hexagonal hinterlands hardly tallied with the realities of Chinese history. In the Taihu Lake basin where the economy was well developed since the Song dynasty, the number of villages or county towns surrounding each county or prefectural capital was not limited to six. Even in terms of geographic position, it never formed into a honeycomb-like structure. In the southwestern mountainous regions where the economy was underdeveloped, going to a standard market would take a whole day so that formation of a hexagonal network was impossible. As for the central position of the capital cities in a macroregion, Professor Qi argued that, although the development of the ancient Chinese capitals was closely related to the development of economy and transportation, many cities became capitals because of their political importance rather than their economic strength. Kaifeng during the Song, for example, was a consumer city in which service trades exceeded those of production. These cities rose and fell according to the political situation. It was difficult to accurately spot changes in the economic development of a region if one based his research only on cities.

In their summaries at the symposium, the chairmen of the two delegations each pointed to a question which divided them. Feuerwerker said that one could sense the presence of an ideological bias against commerce and trade at the symposium. He said, for example, that some people admitted on the one hand that commerce was a positive factor that could lead to the emergence of the sprouts of capitalism. But on the other hand, they always described commerce as a form of exploitation, and this attitude prevailed in their comments. Such an attitude, he said, was against the law of value on which market activities are based. He said, "Let's not condemn the merchants. Instead, we should make a serious study of their activities!" Yan Zhongping maintained that in facing extremely complex historical facts and phenomena, we must discover the laws that govern them, the thread that links them. And this thread is class and class struggle. Without class analysis, it would be very difficult to grasp the essentials in historical research.

Written by Zhuge Ji
Translated by Xing Wenjun

AUTHOR'S NOTE:

The papers presented at the symposium covered a lot of ground. Preparation of this article was rendered even more difficult by lack of complete recordings of the discussions. I hope that participants will forgive any omissions, misunderstandings, or inaccuracies. All corrections and criticisms are welcome.

APPENDIXES AND GLOSSARY

APPENDIX A
SYMPOSIUM PARTICIPANTS

American Delegation

Albert Feuerwerker 费维恺 (Chairman)
Department of History, The University of Michigan

G. William Skinner 施坚雅 (Vice-chairman)
Department of Anthropology, Stanford University

William Atwell 艾维四
School of Oriental and African Studies, University of London

Fu-mei Chang Chen 张富美
Hoover Institution, Stanford University

Jerry Dennerline 邓尔麟
Department of History, Amherst College

Robert Hartwell 郝若贝
Department of History, University of Pennsylvania

Brian E. McKnight 马伯良
Department of History, University of Hawaii

Evelyn S. Rawski 罗斯基
Department of History, University of Pittsburgh

Gilbert Rozman 饶济凡
Department of Sociology, Princeton University

Yeh-chien Wang 王业健
Department of History, Kent State University

Additional American Participants

Beatrice Bartlett 白彬菊
Fairbank Center for East Asian Research, Harvard University

Philip Huang 黄宗智
Department of History, University of California, Los Angeles

Frederic Wakeman, Jr. 魏克曼
Department of History, University of California, Berkeley

Silas Wu 吳秀良
Department of History, Boston College

Chinese Delegation

Yan Zhongping 严中平 (Chairman)
Institute of Economics, CASS

Deng Guangming 邓广铭 (Vice-chairman)
Department of History, Beijing University

Wang Yuquan 王毓铨 (Vice-chairman)
Institute of History, CASS

Bao Yanbang 鲍彦邦
Department of History, Jinan University

Chen Zhen 陈振
Henan Provincial Historical Research Institute

Cheng Yingliu 程应镠
Department of History, Shanghai Teachers' College

Cong Hanxiang 从翰香
Institute of Modern History, CASS

Fan Shuzhi 樊树志
Department of History, Fudan University

Guo Songyi 郭松义
Institute of History, CASS

Hong Huanchun 洪焕椿
Department of History, Nanjing University

Li Wenzhi 李文治
Institute of Economics, CASS

Li Xun 李洵
Department of History, Jilin Normal University

Lin Renchuan 林仁川
Historical Research Institute, Xiamen University

Peng Zeyi 彭泽益
Institute of Economics, CASS

Qi Xia 漆侠
Department of History, Hebei University

Wang Sizhi 王思治
Qing History Research Institute, People's University

Wang Zengyu 王 曾 瑜
Institute of History, CASS

Wei Qingyuan 韦 庆 远
Department of Archives, People's University

Yang Guozhen 杨 国 桢
Department of History, Xiamen University

Ye Xian'en 叶 显 恩
Department of History, Zhongshan University

Additional Chinese Participants

Cao Guilin 曹 桂 林
Institute of History, CASS

Han Hengyu 韩 恒 煜
Institute of History, CASS

Jing Junjian 经 君 健
Institute of Economics, CASS

Ju Deyuan 鞠 德 源
First History Archives, Beijing

Li Jiaju 郦 家 驹
Institute of History, CASS

Liu Yongcheng 刘 永 成
Institute of History, CASS

Luo Ming 罗 明
Qing History Research Institute, People's University

Ran Guangrong 冉 光 荣
Department of History, Sichuan University

Wang Rongsheng 王 戎 笙
Institute of History, CASS

Zhou Baozhu 周 宝 珠
Department of History, Henan Normal University

SCHOLARS MET DURING THE AMERICAN DELEGATION'S TOUR

Nanjing University, Department of History, 8 November 1980

Deng Rui 邓 瑞
Ancient History

Fang Zhiguang 方 之 光
Modern History

Hao Shusheng 郝 树 声
Modern History

Jiang Tao 姜 涛
Graduate student, Modern History

Luo Lun 罗 崙
Ancient History

Qian Xianmin 钱 宽 氏
Graduate student, Modern History

Shi Peihua 石 培 华
Graduate student, Modern History

Wu Yishu 伍 贻 书
Ancient History

Zhang Gaoji 张 高 缉
Ancient History

Zhang Shengming 张 戚 鸣
Graduate student, Modern History

Zhang Yihua 张 升 华
Modern History

Zhou Yanfa 周 衍 发
Modern History

Shanghai Academy of Social Sciences (ShASS), 12 November 1980

Chen Kuangshi 陈 匡 时
Department of History, Fudan University; Chairman, Modern History Research
  Section

Chen Xulu 陈 旭 麓
Department of History, Huadong Shifan University; Chairman, Modern History Research Section

Cheng Yingliu 程 应 镠
Vice-chairman, Department of History, ShASS; Professor, Shanghai Shifan Xueyuan

Fang Shiming 方 诗 铭
Historical Research Institute, ShASS; Chairman, Ancient History Research Section

Lin Qitang 林 其 煋
Historical Research Institute, ShASS; Economics Research Institute

Luo Suwen 罗 素 文
Historical Research Institute, ShASS

Ma Bohuang 马 伯 煌
Professor, Economics Research Institute, ShASS

Meng Qixing 孟 起 兴
Historical Research Institute, ShASS

Tang Zhijun 汤 志 钧
Historical Research Institute, ShASS; Chairman, Modern History Research Section

Wang Shaopu 王 少 普
Historical Research Institute, ShASS

Wang Shoujia 王 守 稼
Historical Research Institute, ShASS

Wang Xi 汪 熙
Professor, Department of History, Fudan University

Wu Guifang 吴 贵 芳
Responsible person, Shanghai Museum, Local History Research Section

Wu Qiandui 吴 乾 兑
Historical Research Institute, ShASS; Modern History Research Section

Xia Dongyuan 夏 东 元
Department of History, Fudan University; Chairman, Modern History Teaching and Research Section

Xu Yuanji 徐 元 基
Historical Research Institute, ShASS; Modern History Research Section

Yang Tingfu 杨 廷 福
Professor, Department of History, Shanghai Jiaoyu Xueyuan

Zhang Zhongli 张 仲 礼
Professor, Economics Research Institute, ShASS

Fudan University, 13 November 1980

Chen Jiang 陈绛
Modern History Teaching and Research Section
Chen Kuangshi 陈匡时
Modern History Teaching and Research Section
Fan Shuzhi 樊树志
Ancient History Teaching and Research Section
Li Huaxing 李华星
History of Political Thought Research Section
Shen Weibin 沈渭滨
Modern History Teaching and Research Section
Sun Zuomin 孙作民
Fudan University Library
Wang Huailiang 汪槐龄
Ancient History Teaching and Research Section
Wang Xi 汪熙
Modern History Teaching and Research Section
Xu Lianda 徐连达
Ancient History Teaching and Research Section
Yang Liqiang 杨立强
Modern History Teaching and Research Section
Zhao Keyao 赵克尧
Ancient History Teaching and Research Section
Zhou Weiyan 周维衍
Historical Geography Research Section

Hangzhou University, 14 November 1980

Chen Qiaoyi 陈桥驿
Huang Shijian 黄时鉴
Jiang Zhaocheng 蒋兆成
Liang Taiji 梁太济
Ma Yuxiang 马裕祥
Wang Sijun 王嗣均
Yan Deyi 严德一

DAILY SYMPOSIUM SCHEDULE AND
POSTSYMPOSIUM ITINERARY FOR THE AMERICAN DELEGATION

Daily Symposium Schedule

26 October 1980

Afternoon: *Opening Ceremony*
    Yan Zhongping, Chairman
    Huan Xiang 宦乡 , Speaker
    Albert Feuerwerker, Response

27 October

Morning: *Rural Social and Political Structure* 农村的社会和政治结构
    (Yan Zhongping, Chairman)

1. "On the Forces of the Jiangnan (South of the Changjiang River) Group" 论明代江南集团势力, by Li Xun (Critic: Jerry Dennerline)

2. "China's Landlord Economy and the Sprouts of Agrarian Capitalism" 论中国地主经济与农业资本主义萌芽, by Li Wenzhi (Critic: Albert Feuerwerker)

3. "A Preliminary Study of the Unofficial Land Sales in Northern Fujian During the Qing Dynasty" 试论清代闽北民间的土地买卖, by Yang Guozhen (Critic: Fu-mei Chang Chen)

Afternoon: *New Research Trends on Popular Culture* 民间文化生活：新的探索
    (Yan Zhongping, Chairman)

1. "Social Structure, Kinship, and Local-Level Politics in Ming and Qing China" 明清社会结构亲族关系及地方政治活动 , by Jerry Dennerline (Critic: Li Wenzhi)

2. "A Report on the Investigation of the Tenant System in Chawan Village, Qimen County, and Mingzhou Village, Xiuning County, of Huizhou" 关于徽州祁门查湾和休宁茗州佃仆制的调查报告 , by Ye Xian'en (Critic: Fu-mei Chang Chen)

3. "Education, Functional Literacy, and Their Economic and Social Effects" 教育，识字力及其对经济和社会的影响, by Evelyn Rawski (Critic: Hong Huanchun)

28 October

<u>Morning:</u>　　　*Population and Urbanization* 人口与都市化
　　　　　　　(Albert Feuerwerker, Chairman)

1. "Two Examples of the Development of Cities in the Song Dynasty" 宋代都市发展两证, by Cheng Yingliu (Critic: Brian McKnight)

2. "Kaifeng Around the Eleventh Century" 十一世纪前后的开封 , by Chen Zhen (Critic: G. William Skinner)

3. "Historical Demography: Sources and Indicators for the Study of the Qing Population" 历史人口学：清代人口研究诸来源与指标 , by Gilbert Rozman (Critic: Chen Zhenhan)

<u>Afternoon:</u>　　*The Agricultural Economy and Property Relations* 农业经济与土地所有制
　　　　　　　(Albert Feuerwerker, Chairman)

1. "The Social Status of Peasants in Chinese History" 论中国历史上农民的身分 , by Wang Yuquan (Critic: Evelyn Rawski)

2. "The Form of Land Rent and Its Evolution During the Song Dynasty" 宋代地租形态及其演变：兼论地价及其地租的关系 , by Qi Xia (Critic: Robert Hartwell)

3. "A Preliminary Analysis of Tenant-Landlord Relationships in Ming and Qing China" 明清之际地主佃农关系试探, by Fu-mei Chang Chen (Critic: Yang Guozhen)

29 October

<u>Morning:</u>　　　*Government and the Economy (I)* 政府与经济的关系 (一)
　　　　　　　(Wang Yuquan, Chairman)

1. "The State and the Economy in Late Imperial China" 宋代以来的中国政府与中国经济 , by Albert Feuerwerker (Critic: Deng Guangming)

2. "The Relationship of the Mercenary System of the Northern Song Period to Social Weaknesses, Poverty, and Agricultural Production" 北宋募兵制度及其与当时积弱积贫和农业生产的关系 , by Deng Guangming (Critic: Brian McKnight)

3. "The System of Tax on Grain Transported from South China Via the Grand Canal During the Ming Dynasty" 明代漕粮制度 , by Bao Yanbang (Critic: Yeh-chien Wang)

Afternoon: *Recess*

30 October

Morning: *Government and the Economy (II)* 政府与经济的关系(二)
              (Deng Guangming, Chairman)

1. "The Rise and Development of the 'Single-Whip' Tax Reform (*yitiaobian fa*)" 一条鞭法的由来与发展 , by Fan Shuzhi (Critic: William Atwell)

2. "Wasteland Reclamation Policies and Achievements During the Reigns of Shunzhi (1644-1661) and Kangxi (1662-1722)" 顺治康熙时期垦荒政策的推行及其成效 , by Guo Songyi (Critic: Evelyn Rawski)

3. "The Secular Movement of Grain Prices in China, ca. 1760-1910" 清代粮价的长期变动 , by Yeh-chien Wang (Critic: Peng Zeyi)

Afternoon: *Regional Marketing Systems and Socioeconomic Development*
              区域贸易范围和社会经济发展
              (Deng Guangming, Chairman)

1. "Marketing Systems and Regional Economies: Their Structure and Development" 市场及区域经济系统的发展 , by G. William Skinner (Critic: Wang Yuquan)

2. "Patterns of Settlement, the Structure of Government, and the Social Transformation of the Chinese Elite, ca. 750-1550" 公元 750-1550 期间中国人口迁移模式，政治结构与官绅阶级的社会蜕变, by Robert Hartwell (Critic: Cheng Yingliu)

3. "The Rise and Fall of the Salt Merchants Along the Huaihe River During the First Half of the Qing Dynasty" 清朝前期两淮盐商的盛衰, by Wang Sizhi and Jin Chengji (Critic: Gilbert Rozman)

31 October

<u>Morning</u>: *Privileged Economic, Social, and Political Groups in Imperial China* 皇朝体制下享有特殊经济，社会和政治利益的集团
(G. William Skinner, Chairman)

1. "Song Legal Privileges" 宋代法律（上的）特权, by Brian McKnight (Critic: Wang Zengyu)

2. "The Rise and Fall of Fan: The Noted Qing Imperial Merchant Family" 清代著名皇商范氏的兴衰, by Wei Qingyuan and Wu Qiyan (Critic: William Atwell)

3. "Private Sea Trade Merchants and the *Wokou* in the Ming Dynasty" 明代私人海上贸易商人, by Lin Renchuan (Critic: William Atwell)

<u>Afternoon</u>: *Handicraft Industry and Capitalist Sprouts* 手工业与资本主义萌芽
(Wang Yuquan, Chairman)

1. "The Development of Industry and Commerce and the Sprouts of Capitalism in Suzhou During the Ming and Qing Dynasties" 明清苏州工商业的发展和资本主义萌芽, by Hong Huanchun (Critic: Jerry Dennerline)

2. The Development of the Handicraft Industry in the First Half of the Qing Dynasty" 清代前期手工业的发展, by Peng Zeyi (Critic: G. William Skinner)

3. "A Preliminary Study of the Development of the Cotton Planting and Textile Industries During the Ming Dynasty" 试述明代植棉和棉纺织业的发展, by Cong Hanxiang (Critic: Yeh-chien Wang)

1 November

<u>Morning</u>: *Money and Foreign Trade* 货币与对外贸易
(G. William Skinner, Chairman)

1. "Some Problems Concerning *Jiaozi* in the Northern Song Period" 关于北宋交子的几个问题, by Wang Zengyu (Critic: Robert Hartwell)

2. "Time and Money: Another Approach to the Periodization of Ming History" 从国内外银产和国际贸易看明史的时代划分, by William Atwell (Critic: Li Xun)

3. "The Opium War and China's Trade with the Western Countries, 1840–1860" 鸦片战争与中西贸易 (1840–1860), by Yan Zhongping (Critic: Albert Feuerwerker)

Postsymposium Itinerary for the American Delegation

2 November. Beijing: Dongling; Mashenqiao; Jixian (periodic market in session, unscheduled stop).

3 November. Beijing: Number One Archive.

4 November. Beijing: Great Wall; Ming Tombs.

5 November. Beijing: Museum of Chinese History. Night train to Nanjing.

6 November. Nanjing: Shuiximen; Mozhouhu; Nanjing Museum (Jiangsu history exhibit).

7 November. Nanjing: site of the Ming imperial palace; Number Two Archive; Zhu Yuanzhang's tomb; Sun Yat-sen's tomb; Shenyang acrobats.

8 November. Nanjing University: report to the Department of History by Albert Feuerwerker and G. William Skinner; university library; history department library and reading room. Yangzi River bridge; Taiping History Museum; South Gate; Drum Tower.

9 November. Train to Suzhou. Suzhou: Zhuozheng Garden; Suzhou Museum; silk factory.

10 November. Suzhou: Tianpingshan (Fan Zhongyan family tombs); Lingyan Gongmu (cemetery); Huqiu; Liu Garden; Beisi Ta (pagoda); Yuanmiaoguan Taoist Temple and market. Train to Shanghai.

11 November. Jiadingxian: Jiading city; Confucian temple (old county school); museum (local history exhibit); Huilong Lake; public garden (Dachangtai Pavilion of the Ningbo Bang, Shanghai); Fahuasi Pagoda; county revolutionary committee headquarters (lunch); site of Ye Pond (where Hou Tongzeng committed suicide). Nanxiangzhen: Guyi Garden; Nanxiang Temple site, pagodas. Shanghai: Yu Garden; Chenghuang Miao (now called Yuyuan Nanchang).

12 November. Shanghai: Shanghai branch of the Chinese Academy of Social Sciences (report on the symposium); Shanghai Municipal Library (rare book section); Shanghai Museum (history section); banquet, Shanghai branch of CASS.

13 November. Shanghai: Fudan University (report to the history department on the symposium); Fudan University library; Shanghai Commission on Trade and Industry reception. Train to Hangzhou.

14 November. Hangzhou: Lingyinsi; Yuewang Miao; Hangzhou Museum (local history exhibit); Hangzhou University Departments of History and Geography (report on the symposium); Shaoxing opera performance.

15 November. Bus to Shaoxing: Xiaoshan (no stop); Geqiao (forty-minute stop); via Zhedong Canal. Shaoxing: Shaoxing Fandian (apparently an old *shuyuan*); Lu Xun Memorial Museum; Lu Xun (Zhou) family residence; Sanwei Shuwu (private school where Lu Xun studied as a boy); Yu Miao; East Lake; meeting with members of the Shaoxing Prefectural Cultural Preservation Committee.

16 November. Bus to Ningbo: Cao'e (ten-minute stop); Guancheng (twenty-minute stop); via Zhenhaixian. Ningbo: Tiantongsi; Wu Fo Zhenmangsi; Xiazhuang village (twenty-minute stop); meeting with members of the Ningbo Historical Society.

17 November. Ningbo: Tianyige Library; Ningbo city tour. Train to Shanghai.

18 November. Departure from China.

APPENDIX D
TWO LIBRARIES

Zhejiang Provincial Library, Hangzhou

On our brief visit to the library we failed to meet He Kuaichang, head of the rare book section, who was out of town, but we were able to talk with assistants about sources and access. The library, with a total of 2 million titles, is divided into two locations. The one we visited is for "old books" (*guji*), which means both *shanben* and pre-1949 periodicals. There are 6,000 titles in all in the general rare book collection, all of them catalogued. In addition to this general collection, the library now houses one special collection of rare books, the remnants of the Jiayetang Library of Nanxun, Wucheng county, Huzhou prefecture. The latter was one of three famous collections in northern Zhejiang in the late Qing period, being the private library of Liu Chenggan. The collection has diminished since then, but what remains is being classified for inclusion in the national union catalogue (*Quan guo guji zongmu*), along with the rest of the Hangzhou holdings. The old Wenlange, which houses a complete copy of the *Siku quanshu* (some of it copied from the Jehol one), is attached.

The library has old printed copies, handwritten copies, and original manuscripts. We saw a few examples, including a hand-copied set of essays by a group of Restoration Society authors of the 1630s. We were told the collection includes *zongpu*, *jiapu*, and *nianpu*, but we were unable to get a sense of the range or volume of these sources. Subcounty gazetteers (*zhen*, *xiang*, and *lizhi*) and local histories in manuscript form, such as those held by the Shanghai Museum and the Shanghai Municipal Library, are not in evidence. Nor are there any special collections of maps or documents, according to our informers. We were told that Japanese researchers have begun to use the collection, and we learned of no restrictions of access comparable to those encountered at the Ming-Qing archive, the Shanghai Municipal Library, or the Nanjing Library.

Tianyige Library, Ningbo

The Tianyige Library in Ningbo is the second of the three great Qing collections in northern Zhejiang (the third being Yuhailou in Rui'an). The private library of the Fan family since the 1560s (see Hummel et al., *Eminent Chinese of the Ch'ing Period*, p. 230), the collection not only contributed 638 titles to the *Siku quanshu* but also received over 10,000 volumes as gifts from the Qianlong emperor in return. Much was lost in the Taiping Rebellion. In 1949, the collection included only 23,000 titles. It has since grown to 300,000, some 80,000 of which are classified as *shanben*, making it the fourth or fifth largest collection in the country.

The last printed catalogue was compiled between 1940 and 1942. A new rare book catalogue has been completed and will be included in the national union catalogue of rare books. The collection suffered no losses during the Cultural Revolution, and new acquisitions include some 50,000-100,000 *juan* donated by private parties.

We asked specifically about subcounty gazetteers, local histories in manuscript form, *jiapu*, and documentary sources like contracts and registers. Subcounty gazetteers and other local histories were unheard of, and the library claims not to collect documents. We were told that *jiapu* have been hard to collect since Liberation, that those that have been collected have not been catalogued, and that most of these have been sent on to the Shanghai Library. Among the older family histories, of which there is a smattering, were *jiapu* of the Fan family—the Tianyige owners, date unknown—and a *zongpu* for the Wan lineage revised by Wan Biao in the late Ming, by Wan Sida in the early Qing, and printed in 1771.

We were permitted by the director, Qiu Sibin, and his assistant, Luo Zhaoping, to rummage through the rare book catalogue and to call up whatever interested us. We saw local gazetteers, a treatise on law, and a number of Ming civil-service examination reports. The latter represented a collection of several dozens, covering a wide range of years, levels of examination, and type of record. They were packed in newspapers dating from the 1930s. They are extremely fragile and will not be available to researchers until they have been restored.

The Tianyige Library gave us a very warm welcome and encouraged us to return. Japanese researchers have begun to work here also.

GLOSSARY

The Glossary includes most of the Chinese names, terms, and book/essay titles mentioned in the text of Parts I-III and Appendix D (names of historical figures, well-known published works, most place names, and commonly recognized terms have been omitted). Characters for the names of the symposium participants and for many of the other scholars mentioned in the text will be found in Appendixes A and B. The numbers in parentheses following each entry below refer to the page(s) on which the item appears.

Romanization (page references)	Characters
bailiang (73)	白粮
baojia (111, 139, 149)	保甲
Beijing Lishi Bowuguan (26)	北京历史博物馆
caoliang (73)	漕粮
chaoben (49)	抄本
Chen Lesu (31)	陈乐素
Chen Zhenhan (38)	陈振汉
Chengde bishu shanzhuang (28)	承德避暑山庄
Chongzeng shiyi daminglü (50)	重增释义大明律
chuanchaoben (49)	传抄本
Daminglü (50)	大明律
dan (141)	担
Di-yi (25)	第一
dianpu (67, 131, 132)	佃仆
diding heyi (88)	地丁合一
ding (122)	丁
dou (141)	斗
duanbai (123)	短陌

178

Duquyuan (77)	杜曲院
Dusheng (77, 78)	杜昇
er dizhu (130)	二地主
fang (80)	坊
Fang Hao (48)	方豪
fangzhi (41, 111)	方志
Faxue yanjiu (44)	法学研究
Fei Xiaotong (19)	费孝通
Fu Yiling (25, 55, 56)	傅衣凌
gangyin (117, 118)	纲引
Gao Heng (45)	高恒
Gao Min (45)	高敏
gaoben (49)	稿本
gongbao (47)	公報
gongsuo (95, 151)	公所
Gu Lu (28)	顾禄
Guancang gaoben mulu (49)	馆藏稿本目録
guanhu (32)	官户
Gudai Shanghai shulüe (28)	古代上海述略
guiyuan (47)	归原
guji (49, 175)	古籍
hang (79)	行
hanggui (95)	行规
He Kuaichang (175)	何槐昌
Huang Xiaozeng (42, 46)	黄嘯曽
huangce (25, 26)	黄册
huangshang (125)	皇商
huce (111)	户册
huiguan (95, 151)	会馆
hukouce (41, 42)	户口册
jia (26, 139)	甲
Jiajing xinli (50)	嘉靖新例
jian (103, 147)	减
jiandang guan (79, 140)	监当官
jiaozi (123, 124, 140)	交子

jiapu (41, 111, 175, 176) 家譜

Jiayetang (Library) (175) 嘉业堂

jie (123) 界

jingchao guan (79) 京朝官

jingshi (61) 经世

Jinmen baojia tushuo (111) 津门保甲图说

juanhao (47) 卷号

jun (94) 郡

juntian junyi (88) 均田均役

junyao (87) 均傜

Kang-Yong-Qian shiqi cheng xiang renmin fankang douzheng ziliao (28) 康雍乾时期城乡人民反抗斗争资料

kehu (32) 客户

Li Hua (28) 李华

Li Min (43) 黎民

Li Xin (48) 李新

Lin Ganquan (5) 林甘泉

Liu Chuyong (27) 刘楚迢

lizhi (175) 里志

lu (137) 路

Lü Zuoxie (26, 28) 吕祚壁

Luo Zhaoping (176) 骆兆平

Ming-Qing Dang'an (25) 明清档案

Ming-Qing yilai Beijing gongshang huiguan beike xuanbian (28) 明清以来北京工商会馆碑刻选编

Minzhu yu fazhi (44) 民主与法制

mulu (32) 目录

Nanjing Bowuguan (26) 南京博物馆

Nanjing daxue tushuguan cang, Guji shanben tushu mulu (48) 南京大学图书馆藏古籍善本图书目录

Nanjing linshi zhengfu (48) 南京临时政府

neishi shi (79) 内侍使

neiwufu (25) 内务府

nianpu (175) 年谱

Ningbo Diqu Lishi Xuehui (28) 宁波地区历史学会

Ningbo Shi Lishi Xuehui (27) 宁波市历史学会

Ouyang Fanxiu (43)	欧阳凡修
pailou (27)	牌楼
peizhu (130)	赔主
piaofa (118)	票法
pu (80)	铺
qian (141)	钱
qianyin (123)	钱引
qing (103, 147)	请
Qing xian cuntu (111)	青县村图
Qingshi Yanjiusuo (25, 28)	清史研究所
Qingshigao xingfazhi zhujie (44)	清史稿刑法志注解
Qiu Sibin (28, 176)	邱嗣斌
Qu Tongzu (19, 44)	瞿同祖
Quan guo guji zongmu (175, 176)	全国古籍总目
Quan Hansheng (63)	全汉升
Renmin gongan (44)	人民公安
Renmin jiancha (44)	人民检察
Renmin sifa (44)	人民司法
shanben (175, 176)	善本
Shanghai beike ziliao xuanji (28)	上海碑刻资料选辑
Shaoxing Xian Wenwu Baoguan Weiyuanhui (27)	绍兴县文物保管委员会
Shehui kexue zhanxian (45)	社会科学战线
sheng (94)	省
sheng yige hao (38)	生一个好
shi (73)	石
shougao (49)	手稿
shoushengpo (41)	收生婆
shu (103, 147)	赎
shuichang (144)	税场
shuipu (144)	税铺
Siku quanshu (175, 176)	四库全书
Song huiyao jigao (140)	宋会要辑稿
tanding rudi (88)	摊丁入地
Tang Biao (47)	唐彪
Tianyige (Library) (26, 28, 49, 174, 176)	天一阁

182

MICHIGAN MONOGRAPHS IN CHINESE STUDIES

No. 2. *The Cultural Revolution: 1967 in Review*, four essays by Michel Oksenberg, Carl Riskin, Robert Scalapino, and Ezra Vogel.

No. 3. *Two Studies in Chinese Literature*, by Li Chi and Dale Johnson.

No. 4. *Early Communist China: Two Studies*, by Ronald Suleski and Daniel Bays.

No. 5. *The Chinese Economy, ca. 1870-1911*, by Albert Feuerwerker.

No. 7. *The Treaty Ports and China's Early Modernization: What Went Wrong?* by Rhoads Murphey.

No. 8. *Two Twelfth Century Texts on Chinese Painting*, by Robert J. Maeda.

No. 9. *The Economy of Communist China, 1949-1969*, by Chu-yuan Cheng.

No. 10. *Educated Youth and the Cultural Revolution in China*, by Martin Singer.

No. 11. *Premodern China: A Bibliographical Introduction*, by Chun-shu Chang.

No. 12. *Two Studies on Ming History*, by Charles O. Hucker.

No. 13. *Nineteenth-Century China: Five Imperialist Perspectives*, selected by Dilip Basu and edited by Rhoads Murphey.

No. 14. *Modern China, 1840-1972: An Introduction to Sources and Research Aids*, by Andrew J. Nathan.

No. 15. *Women in China: Studies in Social Change and Feminism*, edited by Marilyn B. Young.

No. 17. *China's Allocation of Fixed Capital Investment, 1952-1957*, by Chu-yuan Cheng.

No. 18. *Health, Conflict, and the Chinese Political System*, by David M. Lampton.

No. 19. *Chinese and Japanese Music-Dramas*, edited by J. I. Crump and William P. Malm.

No. 21. *Rebellion in Nineteenth-Century China*, by Albert Feuerwerker.

No. 22. *Between Two Plenums: China's Intraleadership Conflict, 1959-1962*, by Ellis Joffe.

No. 23. *"Proletarian Hegemony" in the Chinese Revolution and the Canton Commune of 1927*, by S. Bernard Thomas.

No. 24. *Chinese Communist Materials at the Bureau of Investigation Archives, Taiwan*, by Peter Donovan, Carl E. Dorris, and Lawrence R. Sullivan.

No. 25. *Shanghai's Old-Style Banks (Ch'ien-chuang), 1800-1935*, by Andrea Lee McElderry.

No. 26. *The Sian Incident: A Pivotal Point in Modern Chinese History*, by Tien-wei Wu.

MICHIGAN ABSTRACTS OF CHINESE AND JAPANESE WORKS ON CHINESE HISTORY

Michigan Monographs and Abstracts available from:

Center for Chinese Studies
The University of Michigan
104 Lane Hall (Publications)
Ann Arbor, Michigan 48109 USA